Exploring Administrative Decision-Making in Public Education

"This compelling book delves into the crucial intersection of public K-12 education and negligence, providing invaluable and novel insights for school personnel. With a keen examination of the unique challenges and responsibilities faced within the public education system, Godett and Nobile provide an indispensable guide for fostering a safe and accountable environment for both students, staff, and school administrators."
—Chris Yarrell, Education Attorney, *Center for Law & Education*

"As a former high school principal I find that the authors' approach to the ever-evolving issue of negligence in public education is not only very timely (thanks, for example, to the inclusion of negligence regarding technology) but extremely thought-provoking as well. Their work provoked me to think of applications not only in the context of my school experience, but also beyond that as they might apply to more comprehensive questions. I found myself reexamining long-held personal notions and ideas about negligence, my role and my exposure. Each chapter challenged me to pause, reflect, and apply. I particularly enjoyed the balance between examples in case law and hypothetical scenarios. With decades of experience as an educator, it's not often that a work makes me sit up and take a fresh look at my established ideas. These authors have done that."
—Tom Welch, *former high school principal and current education consultant*

Godett and Nobile use the concept of Next-Gen Negligence to precisely explain how, through the logic of Students for Fair Admission v. Harvard, conservatives are turning the very idea of equity upside down at this very moment. More importantly, they use the Next Gen Negligence concept to create a roadmap for taking the Equal Protection Clause back, hopefully to better the lives of our most vulnerable students."
—Stephen Himes, Co-Founder and Head of Advising, *Storyboards College Admission Portfolios, a Nationwide College Admissions Counseling Firm*

Beth Godett • Liana M. Nobile

Exploring Administrative Decision-Making in Public Education

The Negligence Evolution

Beth Godett
Education Law and Policy
Boston College
Chestnut Hill, MA, USA

Rider University
Lawrenceville, NJ, USA

Liana M. Nobile
Attorney in Jersey City
Maron Marvel Bradley Anderson & Tardy LLC
Jersey City, NJ, USA

ISBN 978-3-031-58781-8   ISBN 978-3-031-58782-5 (eBook)
https://doi.org/10.1007/978-3-031-58782-5

© The Editor(s) (if applicable) and The Author(s), under exclusive license to Springer Nature Switzerland AG 2024

This work is subject to copyright. All rights are solely and exclusively licensed by the Publisher, whether the whole or part of the material is concerned, specifically the rights of translation, reprinting, reuse of illustrations, recitation, broadcasting, reproduction on microfilms or in any other physical way, and transmission or information storage and retrieval, electronic adaptation, computer software, or by similar or dissimilar methodology now known or hereafter developed.
The use of general descriptive names, registered names, trademarks, service marks, etc. in this publication does not imply, even in the absence of a specific statement, that such names are exempt from the relevant protective laws and regulations and therefore free for general use.
The publisher, the authors and the editors are safe to assume that the advice and information in this book are believed to be true and accurate at the date of publication. Neither the publisher nor the authors or the editors give a warranty, expressed or implied, with respect to the material contained herein or for any errors or omissions that may have been made. The publisher remains neutral with regard to jurisdictional claims in published maps and institutional affiliations.

Cover credit : Pattern © Melisa Hasan

This Palgrave Macmillan imprint is published by the registered company Springer Nature Switzerland AG.
The registered company address is: Gewerbestrasse 11, 6330 Cham, Switzerland

If disposing of this product, please recycle the paper.

*To Fred, my true partner,
whose love and support make it possible for me to pursue my dreams.
To Mike and Joel, my favorite (and only) sons,
on whom I can always rely to call things as they see them.
And to Art, my friend and mentor,
who inspires me to look to the future with hope.
−Beth*

*For all of my teachers, both in and out of the classroom,
but especially Mom, Raquel, Shane,
Dr. Beth Godett, Mrs. Bonnie McQuarie, Mrs. Pat Ryan, Mr. Tony
Saraceno, Mrs. Sharon Sweeney, Professor Karen Schmelzkopf, Professor
Charles Sullivan, and Judge Dennis R. O'Brien, J.S.C., Ret.
—I wouldn't be the lawyer and person I am without each and every one of
you holding my hand along the way.
−Liana*

Acknowledgments

With thanks and appreciation to those educators, attorneys, colleagues, family, and friends who provided us with inspiration and feedback!

Fred Godett
Joel Godett
Mike Godett
Luis Guzman
Steve Himes
Jana Lee
MaryEllen Maatman
Shane McDougall
Lisa Maslankowski
Maren Maslankowski
Raquel Muniz
Gerri Nobile
Chris Yarrell
Tom Welch

Contents

Part I	Defining Negligence in Public Schools	1
1	Preface: A Note from the Authors	3
2	Traditional Understandings of Negligence	7
3	Administrators' Responsibilities Regarding Negligence	17
4	Negligence and the Right to an Education	27
Part II	Introducing "Next-Gen Negligence"	37
5	Defining "Next-Gen Negligence"	39
Part III	Challenges to the Status Quo	47
6	Challenges Posed by Public Policy	49
7	Challenges Posed by Parents	63

Part IV Next-Gen Negligence in Context — 73

8 Next-Gen Negligence and Free Expression — 75

9 Next-Gen Negligence and Equity — 87

10 Next-Gen Negligence and Students' Unique Learning Needs — 101

11 Next-Gen Negligence and Mental Health — 109

12 Next-Gen Negligence and Technology — 121

13 Next-Gen Negligence and Governance — 131

14 Next-Gen Negligence and Unexpected Challenges — 139

Part V Next-Gen Negligence Going Forward — 155

15 Next-Gen Negligence and the Future of Public Education — 157

16 Postscript: Another Note from the Authors — 169

Case Index — 173

Subject Index — 177

About the Authors

Beth Godett brings 35 years of public school experience to her writing including that of a teacher, principal, curriculum director, assistant superintendent, and superintendent. Especially relevant to this publication is that she attained her J.D. as a start to a new professional chapter in her life and embarked on a career as an adjunct professor of education law and policy. Using her school practitioner experience as a filter through which to view the law has provided her with unique and practical insight which proves valuable to her readers.

Beth is known for her presentations at national and international conferences which challenge participants to think differently and critically about court rulings and the legal structure within which public education operates. She has authored articles that look to the future of learning and schooling from a practical perspective intended to foster hope amid a rapidly changing landscape. Her book, *Toward the Bigger Half: Equity in Public Education*, was published in 2024.

Liana Nobile vigorously defends her clients in premises liability disputes and provides advice on insurance coverage matters. Before becoming a defense attorney, Liana was an attorney at a plaintiff's personal injury firm. Her experience on both sides of the aisle has given her useful insight into resolving cases efficiently.

Following her graduation from Seton Hall Law, Liana clerked for the Honorable Dennis J. O'Brien, J.S.C. (Ret.) while he was still on the bench in the Monmouth County Superior Court in New Jersey. This invaluable experience set her up for a successful career as a litigator.

Liana has previously spoken as a guest lecturer on the implications of recent Supreme Court cases on the education industry and on negligence in the school and education setting. She frequently blogs about current legal trends and hot topics on JD Supra and has also spoken as a guest on a legal podcast through Learn Formula.

When not at work, Liana can be found taking in a Broadway show in New York City or spending time with her husband and their golden retriever, Hercules.

LIST OF TABLES

Table 1.1	Identifying negligence	5
Table 2.1	Using the elements to determine negligence	10
Table 6.1	Key policy issues and corresponding levels of liability	59
Table 7.1	A sampling of constitutional guarantees of education by state	67

PART I

Defining Negligence in Public Schools

CHAPTER 1

Preface: A Note from the Authors

Abstract Chapter 1 introduces readers to the inspiration for and purpose of this book, setting out its importance as a guide for school administrators. It encourages readers to begin thinking about liability for negligence from different perspectives and to consider that an important legal aspect of their practice can evolve to take on new meaning.

Keywords Inflection point · Negligence · Talking points

Dear Reader,

This book is written to address a topic of great importance and ever-growing concern at a time President Biden refers to as an "inflection point in history…where the decisions we make today are going to affect the course of our world for the next several decades, for certain" (Biden 2023). President Biden sees the inflection point as many things including climate change and emerging technologies. We, too, see many things happening which may be considered inflection points, turning points, or points from which there may be no turning back. As regards public schooling there is no question that seismic shifts are occurring in the tectonic plates we have always taken for granted as solidly in place.

Public schools have long been viewed as the foundation of a child's education with certain guarantees coming from case law and legislative

© The Author(s), under exclusive license to Springer Nature Switzerland AG 2024
B. Godett, L. M. Nobile, *Exploring Administrative Decision-Making in Public Education*,
https://doi.org/10.1007/978-3-031-58782-5_1

entitlements. Whether changes appearing to impact public education today are true inflection points remains to be seen, and they are among the themes we will explore relative to an administrator's liability for negligence.

We do not intend for this monograph to provide legal advice. We are neither your attorneys nor your school administrators. Yet we believe our experience in both areas can offer helpful insights into the ever-widening range of responsibilities administrators hold relative to the operation of schools and school stakeholders.

Probably one of the most important legal issues to discuss regarding public education is negligence, underplayed yet omnipresent as a potential liability for school administrators. This is because negligence easily joins hands with other laws and becomes the basis for causes of action extending beyond its defined elements of duty, breach, and "but-for" or proximate causation of an injury. Negligence is growing as an area of interest and concern as our world and our relationships with institutions and the people around us evolve. This begs consideration of whether negligence as a looming threat is leading to an exodus of talented administrators and teachers from their positions as dedicated public servants.

Just to scratch the surface, we ask you to consider a wide variety of ways negligence can occur that are listed on the chart that follows (see Table 1.1). The potential exists for categories to overlap with nuanced illustrations.

The chart raises questions:

- Must the administrator's action or inaction be deliberate to be deemed negligent?
- Is there a consistent standard against which negligence can be measured?
- Are there actions that might be considered as negligent by some and not by others based upon an administrator's wide-ranging duties to various student populations and district stakeholders?

We invite you to refer back to this chart as our chapters unfold to appreciate the complexity of this seemingly simple concept. We also encourage you to read the chapters as they follow rather than in isolation. This will help you consider the talking points relative to negligence in your districts and aid in how to have important conversations with those to whom you owe a duty in your position as an administrator.

In the chapters that follow we will provide statements defining elements of the law; some history and case law explaining how public

Table 1.1 Identifying negligence

Category	Description
Intentional negligence/willful negligence	• Demonstrated by deliberate indifference to a situation • Attached to priorities or balance—however misguided
Unintentional negligence—something that might also be called "blind" negligence (or "blinder" negligence)	• Attached to priorities or balance resulting from unintended consequences or an action's effect • A failure of sensitivity to individual needs
Unanticipated negligence	• Failure to see past the details of a situation • Caused by the actions of others beyond an administrator's control
Hidden negligence	• Negligence masked by other unlawful acts, whether deliberately or unintentionally—nevertheless, a peripheral cause of something unfavorable that has occurred
Shared negligence	• Negligence on the part of one snowballs to include others • Can include both deliberate and unintentional negligent acts and implicate those involved to varying degrees • Ultimately, the administrator may be responsible
Historical negligence	• Negligence over time whose impact continues to affect a student or group of students in any number of ways
Traumatic negligence	• Self-associative negligence resulting in a disassociative response • Something in the administrator's own past causes them to become less objective or effective in addressing responsibilities
Institutional/cultural negligence	• Where the district or school culture facilitates, imposes, or enforces negligence
Ethical disconnect negligence	• When the administrator is forced to serve in a position where the laws do not correspond with their administrative ethics and/or violates their integrity

education came to be where it is currently in terms of negligence; examples, where appropriate, of both hypothetical and real situations involving negligence that require you to reflect on your own practice; and questions to inspire you, dear reader, to think about the possibilities where administrators can incur liability under what we are calling "next-gen negligence."

Wrapped into all of this is the very serious consideration of whether the core legal elements of negligence have expanded in scope in recent years and whether they will evolve or change in years to come. To whom have duties been owed in the past? Has that changed? What constitutes an injury? These are areas ripe for discussion! We only ask that you recognize what we provide in the chapters that follow is not an exhaustive list of every area where an administrator could encounter liability for negligence. Anyone can sue anybody for anything anywhere or at any time (even if it's considered a frivolous lawsuit)!

Ultimately, our discussion may be unable to conclude with certainty whether the elements of negligence are definitively evolving with regard to public education. Is what we introduce as next-gen negligence merely a symptom of a society in flux impacting an organization traditionally accepted as resistant to change? Or is it the harbinger of another inflection point, adding public education to President Biden's list along with climate change and emerging technologies?

Join us as we initiate the conversation!

Reference

Biden, J. (2023, March 29). *Remarks by President Biden at the Summit for Democracy Virtual Plenary on Democracy Delivering on Global Challenges* [Speech transcript]. The White House. https://www.whitehouse.gov/briefing-room/speeches-remarks/2023/03/29/remarks-by-president-biden-at-the-summit-for-democracy-virtual-plenary-on-democracy-delivering-on-global-challenges/

CHAPTER 2

Traditional Understandings of Negligence

Abstract Chapter 2 sets forth a basic explanation of negligence, both through its elements as a common law tort and, also, as it applies to education through the responsibilities of a public school administrator. This chapter presents a legal primer to help administrators develop an understanding of common law negligence and where it fits with their practice. It provides scenarios for the reader to contemplate, complete with questions prompting consideration of actual cases detailed within the chapter.

Keywords Traditional negligence • Tort • Common law negligence • Elements • Reasonably prudent person

In order to understand the concept of "next-gen negligence," it is critical to first have a good foundational understanding of what traditional negligence is and why it is so important in a school law forum. Negligence, at its heart, is a tort (a civil wrong) that is actionable in a civil court of law.

Before delving into a discussion about negligence, it is first necessary to distinguish a civil wrong from other types of law with which we may be more familiar. In the most general terms, there are three broad categories we can think of when we think about the law: criminal law, family law, and civil law.

Criminal law can be thought of simply as "the government versus you." This is what comes to most people's minds when they think of the law, lawyers, courtrooms, courtroom dramas, etc. For those lacking intimate familiarity with law such as non-lawyers and non-legal professionals, criminal law is the easiest to conceptualize when thinking about the legal process. It is what we see most frequently in the media and pop culture.

Again, speaking in the most general of terms, criminal law involves the government (the prosecution) bringing a case against someone who has committed a crime and broken a law (the defendant). In criminal law the government bears the burden of proof, which is where we get the concept of "innocent until *proven* guilty." In criminal cases, the prosecution must prove their case beyond a reasonable doubt, which is an incredibly high burden. If they fail to do so, they lose the case.

Family law is probably the second most common way the general public can relate to the law, lawyers, and courtrooms. Family law encompasses divorces, custody, adoption, and other matters that fall under the broad umbrella category of "family." Family law can be thought of as "you versus you." For purposes of this book, specifically, we will not examine family law in depth other than to acknowledge here that it exists and is another way our legal system operates.

Finally, civil law is the third general category under which American jurisprudence falls. Civil law can be thought of as "you versus me." It is easy to confuse civil and criminal law. For example, under civil law, a person can have violated a statute or law and been found liable; however, the government may not necessarily be the entity bringing the lawsuit. The suit could have been brought by a private person—one private person versus another private person: you versus me. While most people do not have a ready understanding or familiarity with civil law, should you ever find yourself involved in a lawsuit, there is a very good possibility it will be a civil lawsuit because civil law is the venue for all personal injury lawsuits (car accidents, trips/slips and falls, premises liability, toxic tort personal injury cases, etc.), breach of contract cases, and other situations where a private person has wronged another giving rise to a cause of action. Civil cases involve a plaintiff making allegations that the defendant's action caused the plaintiff to suffer harm.

In civil law, the plaintiff sits in the same shoes as the government/prosecution in a criminal case in that the plaintiff bears the burden of proof. However, in civil law, the burden of proof is significantly lower than that in a criminal matter. In proving a civil case, the plaintiff must establish that the defendant caused the harm by "a preponderance of the evidence," which, again in the most general of terms, means that if the fact finder determines that the defendant was more likely than not liable, the plaintiff wins the day. If the plaintiff succeeds in establishing this burden of proof, the defendant is found "liable to the plaintiff" (but not "guilty" as guilty/not guilty is terminology used only in criminal cases, not civil).

Civil law often involves one private person accusing another private person of committing what is known as a tort. The legal definition of "tort" is "an act or omission that gives rise to injury or harm to another and amounts to a civil wrong for which courts impose liability" (Legal Information Institute, Tort, n.d.-b). The person said to have committed a tort is known as a "tortfeasor."

It may be helpful to think of "torts" as the civil corollary to crimes in that they are little wrongs or harms that aren't quite crimes but may be violations of statutes or common law. If someone is found to have committed a tort, they are said to be liable to the plaintiff. There are many different torts—defamation, assault, trespass to land, conversion of property, false imprisonment, nuisance, wrongful death, breach of contract, and many more—but a tort that is seen most frequently and is often at the heart of litigation involving the public school system is the tort of negligence. This chapter will discuss negligence and how a tortfeasor may be found liable for committing the tort of negligence in a civil court of law.

There are two types of negligence: negligence per se and common law negligence. Negligence per se is where a person violates a duty created by statute or administrative regulation. Common law negligence derives from custom, court decisions, and judicial precedent versus statutes and laws (Thomson Reuters, n.d.).

Negligence per se occurs when the plaintiff falls into a class of people protected by a duty statutorily imposed upon a defendant and the defendant violates the statute or administrative regulation enacted to prevent the type of injury suffered by the plaintiff (Legal Information Institute, Negligence per se, n.d.-a).

While it is possible that teachers, administrators, and other public school players may find themselves dealing with a case involving negligence per se, it is much more likely that any litigation arising in the public school setting will involve common law negligence. Accordingly, this book will mostly discuss common law negligence and how it is being reinterpreted, morphed into, and enmeshed with negligence per se in light of recent Supreme Court ("SCOTUS") opinions, various state law issues, and the "court of public opinion." Therefore, when we use the term "negligence," we are referring to "common law negligence," unless specifically stated otherwise.

To fully understand common law negligence and how it is evolving today, it is imperative to examine the existing body of case law and how we expect these existing legal precedents to be interpreted and applied going forward. It is also important to consider the judicial makeup of the various courts acting on these legal precedents.

Negligence, whether contemplating it in a negligence per se setting or in a common law setting, has four elements. It is an "and" test, not an "or" test, so in order for a plaintiff to succeed in a negligence case, they must establish each and every element of the test by a preponderance of the evidence. The elements of negligence are: (1) duty, (2) breach, (3) causation, and (4) damages (also referred to as injury). Said differently, for a plaintiff to succeed in a negligence case, they must prove by a preponderance of the evidence that the defendant owed them a *duty* of care; that the defendant *breached* that duty of care; and, finally, that the breach of that duty of care *caused* them to suffer *damages*. It may be helpful to visualize negligence as follows (see Table 2.1).

As you can see from the questions above, because negligence is an "and" test, the plaintiff must prove each and every one of the four elements by a preponderance of the evidence to be successful. If they fail on even one of the prongs, they fail globally.

In order to fully explore the elements of negligence, let's say our Plaintiff Paula is walking in a grocery store and falls down while in the store. Will Plaintiff Paula succeed in bringing a negligence case against the grocery store?

Table 2.1 Using the elements to determine negligence

Was the defendant negligent?
Did the defendant owe the plaintiff a duty of care?
  No→There is no negligence.
  Yes→(continue)
Did the defendant breach the duty of care owed?
  No→There is no negligence.
  Yes→(continue)
Did the plaintiff sustain an injury?
  No→There is no negligence.
  Yes→(continue)
Did the breach of duty *cause the injury/damages*?
  No→There is no negligence.
  Yes→Plaintiff wins.

2 · TRADITIONAL UNDERSTANDINGS OF NEGLIGENCE 11

Consider each of the following scenarios:

Scenario one:

Plaintiff Paula is walking in a grocery store and trips and falls over her own shoelace. Will she succeed in bringing a negligence claim against the grocery store? No.

Here, the grocery store did not owe Plaintiff Paula a duty to remind her to keep her shoelaces tied. Therefore, Plaintiff Paula will not be successful in bringing a negligence lawsuit against the grocery store in this scenario.

Scenario two:

Plaintiff Paula is walking in a grocery store and slips and falls on an old brown banana peel in the produce aisle and breaks her ankle. Will she succeed in bringing a negligence claim against the grocery store? Yes. Plaintiff Paula can show that the grocery store owed her a duty to keep the floors clean and free of slippery substances, that the grocery store breached the duty to do so by allowing the slippery substance to be on the floor, and that the slippery substance's existence caused her to slip and fall. She will also be able to show that by falling on the slippery substance (causation) she broke her ankle (damages).

Scenario three:

Plaintiff Paula is walking in a grocery store and sees a section of an aisle that was recently mopped and is blocked off with ropes/barricades and "caution wet floor" signs. Plaintiff Paula decides to walk beyond the barricades/ropes anyway and in doing so, she slips and falls, breaking her ankle. Will she succeed in bringing a negligence claim against the grocery store? Likely not.

Without getting too much into an analysis of the situation, it is very likely that although Plaintiff Paula will be able to prove that the grocery store owed her a duty to provide a safe walking space, it is equally likely that the grocery store will be able to prove that it did so by putting up caution wet floor signs and roping off the area that had been mopped, thereby fulfilling its duty to Plaintiff Paula. In this scenario, although Plaintiff Paula will be able to show that the grocery store owed her a duty, the analysis will stop there because there has been no breach of that duty.

Scenario four:

Plaintiff Paula is walking in a grocery store and sees a section of an aisle that was recently mopped, but the person who did the mopping forgot to put up the wet floor sign and barricades to keep Plaintiff Paula and other customers away from the freshly mopped area. Plaintiff Paula's shoelace is open. She safely navigates out of the wet floor area only to trip and fall over her open shoelace, breaking her ankle in the process. Will she succeed in bringing a negligence claim against the grocery store? Likely not.

Here, even though Plaintiff Paula may be able to show that the grocery store owed her a duty to keep her walking path safe and failed to do so by failing to put up caution wet floor signs and barricades, her fall was not caused by the wet floor—it was caused by her own open shoelace. In this scenario, the grocery store would likely win this case because Plaintiff Paula cannot establish the "causation" prong by a preponderance of the evidence.

Scenario five:

Plaintiff Paula is walking in a grocery store and walks through a section of an aisle that was recently mopped where the person who did the mopping forgot to put up the wet floor sign and barricades. Plaintiff Paula slips and falls on the wet floor. However, Plaintiff Paula is lucky because even though she fell, she was not hurt in any way and was able to get up and finish her shopping. Will Plaintiff Paula succeed in bringing a negligence claim against the grocery store? Likely not.

Here, while Plaintiff Paula can prove that the grocery store owed her a duty to keep the floor safe and not slippery, that it breached that duty by permitting the slippery substance to exist on the floor, and that the slippery substance caused her to fall, she cannot prove that she suffered any damages as a result. Therefore, she will not likely win this case as she has not proven all elements of negligence with a preponderance of the evidence.

When considering whether a defendant has been negligent or not, courts consider whether a similar person, acting under similar circumstances, would have acted in the same way. It must be an apples to apples comparison, not apples to oranges. This standard is called the "reasonably prudent [person]." In thinking about the grocery store scenarios with Plaintiff Paula, a court will consider whether the grocery store was negligent by considering whether a reasonably prudent grocer mopping a floor would have acted the same way as the hypothetical grocer from the scenarios, above. A court would not consider, for example, whether a reasonable car salesman would have acted the same way in mopping the floor at a car dealership. More simply, in negligence cases, like is compared to like.

This theory is true, too, in a public school K-12 setting. In a negligence case in a public school setting, the fact finder would not be tasked with determining whether a principal was negligent by considering the actions that a kindergarten teacher might take in the same circumstances—rather you would consider a reasonably prudent principal if the case was brought against a principal, a reasonably prudent kindergarten teacher if the case was brought against a kindergarten teacher, a reasonably prudent librarian if the case was brought against a librarian, a reasonably prudent board member if the case was brought against a board member, and so on.

Common types of negligence cases in general include personal injury cases such as trips and falls, slips and falls, breach of contract, and automobile accidents, among others. One such landmark case receiving national attention and dealing with negligence is *Liebeck v. McDonald's* (1994), often referred to as "The McDonald's Coffee Case."

In this case, Plaintiff Stella Liebeck was severely burned when hot McDonald's coffee spilled in her lap. Although the news at the time reported on this matter in a way that made it seem ridiculous and even frivolous, in reality, the coffee was so hot that it caused Ms. Liebeck to sustain third-degree burns through her clothing in only three seconds over 16% of her body, including to her inner thighs and genitalia. The burns were so severe that her skin burned away down to her muscle and fatty tissue requiring an eight-day hospitalization and skin grafts, among other treatments, for a recovery that lasted two years. Her attorneys were able to successfully prove that McDonald's acted negligently by serving coffee at a temperature 30–40 degrees hotter than that served by other companies, and at a temperature that could cause severe burns within three seconds of skin contact (Burtka, n.d.).

In another landmark negligence case, *Grimshaw v. Ford Motor Co.* (1981), often referred to as "The Ford Pinto Case," a Ford Pinto driven by Lilly Gray stalled when she entered a merge lane on a California highway. Her Pinto was then rear-ended by another car, causing the Pinto's gas tank to rupture and the Pinto to explode. Ms. Gray passed away, and her passenger, Richard Grimshaw, a 13-year-old boy, suffered extensive burns requiring numerous operations. The Grimshaws and Grays sued Ford for negligence, and discovery revealed internal Ford documents showing that Ford had crash-tested the Pinto over 40 times before it went to market and that during each and every test the fuel tank erupted at speeds over 25 miles per hour causing a risk of fire. Although Ford had investigated and identified various safety solutions at nominal costs to the company, none was used in the final production of the Pinto. The trial resulted in substantial damages awarded to the plaintiffs (American Museum of Tort Law, n.d.).

Negligence lawsuits arise not only in scenarios such as those in *Liebeck* and *Grimshaw*, but often in the public school setting as well. Consider this real-life example, *J.R. v. Hudson County Schools of Technology* (HUD-L-3406-17). This is a case Liana litigated, and the details in the next several paragraphs are drawn from her personal experience with this case. Here, J.R. was a high school student taking a gym class. J.R.'s class took place in the school gymnasium with a capacity for 135 students. At the same time J.R.'s class was held in the gymnasium, three other classes were held in the same space. Each class had between 21 and 24 students in them, with no more than 70 students in the space, total, not accounting for absences.

In *J.R. v. Hudson County Schools of Technology*, while the groups were taught separately for the majority of the class period, each with their own teacher in distinct areas of the gymnasium, the gym teachers chose to conduct the warm-ups together to make use of the full gymnasium. During the class period at issue, the teachers decided that warm-ups included a High-Intensity Interval Training (HIIT) run where the students started out walking in one direction around the perimeter of the gym and when the teacher's whistle sounded once, the students were instructed to run; when the whistle sounded twice, the students were instructed to walk.

J.R. was looking down at her phone while doing the HIIT run and she in fact decided not to run at all, only ever walking during the exercise even when the teacher's whistle blew once to signal running. As she was walking with her head down looking at the phone, a student who was fully participating in the exercise needed to run out of J.R.'s path of travel because this student was moving at a faster pace. In doing so, the second student crossed in front of J.R.

J.R. failed to see the running student cross in front of her because she was looking at her phone. As a result, J.R. tripped and fell over the running student's feet, and the fall caused her to twist and break her ankle.

The teacher assigned to J.R.'s class had briefly stepped into his office when J.R. fell, which was across the gym from where the incident happened. The three other teachers were positioned around the perimeter of the gym to supervise the accident, but J.R. fell between two of them. The teachers were stagnant, not circling the gym while the HIIT run took place. J.R. sued the school for negligence alleging: (1) the gym was overcrowded; (2) J.R.'s teacher failed to supervise the HIIT run; and (3) the HIIT run was not appropriate for this class.

Consider the following:

- Can J.R. succeed on her claim for negligence?
- What elements of negligence can J.R. succeed on? Make an argument for and against each element.
- What could the teachers have done differently, if anything?

In the actual case, J.R. did not succeed in her claim for negligence. The fact finder determined that although the teachers and school, generally, owed J.R. a duty to provide a safe gym class, the teachers and school had not breached this duty. In reaching this conclusion, the fact finder considered that the capacity was far below maximum and that even though J.R.'s teacher stepped away at the moment she fell, there was adequate supervision by the other teachers. The fact finder concluded further that J.R.'s own negligence, being on her phone and refusing to participate in the exercise as designed, caused the accident. (*J.R. v. Hudson County Schools of Technology*).

Personal injury cases are not the only way that public schools encounter negligence. Often, negligence is pled, among other causes of action, in bullying and harassment cases. It is not always a student plaintiff in these cases—teachers and administrators can and often do bring claims of negligence against school districts, other teachers or administrators, the school board, and other district employees based on the discrete facts of their claim. Harassment and bullying cases alike are analyzed under state laws against discrimination (LAD). Even though most LAD's elements are written in a way so as to apply to an employment situation, bullying cases are analyzed under analogous prongs applied through the same law.

At this point in this introductory chapter, you may be asking yourself "why are we talking about negligence now?" First, negligence is a very broad umbrella under which a plaintiff can bring a lawsuit. Next, the actual elements of negligence are likely not going anywhere: to sue for negligence, a plaintiff will still need to prove that a breach of a duty caused them to suffer damages. Something to consider is whether the plaintiffs (traditionally those directly involved in the school system—students, teachers, administrators, and other Board of Education employees) and the duties owed may be evolving in light of recent SCOTUS opinions, new state laws and approved curricula, and the court of public opinion. This book aims to provide a roadmap for administrators in predicting, preparing for, and handling instances of negligence that do not fit squarely into the traditional framework commonly used to contemplate negligence cases. This "next-gen negligence" is something for which we can prepare.

REFERENCES

American Museum of Tort Law. (n.d.). *Grimshaw v. Ford Motor Co., 1981*. https://www.tortmuseum.org/ford-pinto/

Burtka, A.T. (n.d.). *The hot coffee case*. American Museum of Tort Law. https://www.tortmuseum.org/liebeck-v-mcdonalds/

Grimshaw v. Ford Motor Co., 119 Cal App 3d 757, 174 Cal Rptr 348 (1981).

J.R. v. Hudson County Schools of Technology (HUD-L-3406-17). (This case was denied cert by the New Jersey Supreme Court, see Kerton ex rel J.R. v. Hudson Cty., 244 N.J. 356 (2020).).

Liebeck v. McDonald's Restaurants, 1995 WL 360309, (D.C.N.M. 1994). Cited in Quimbee. https://www.quimbee.com/cases/liebeck-v-mcdonald-s-restaurants

Legal Information Institute. (n.d.-a). *Negligence per se*. Cornell Law School. negligence per se | Wex | US Law | LII / Legal Information Institute.

Legal Information Institute. (n.d.-b). *Tort*. Cornell Law School. https://www.law.cornell.edu/wex/tort

Thomson Reuters. (n.d.). *Common law: Defining what it is and what you need to know*. https://legal.thomsonreuters.com/en/insights/articles/what-is-common-law.

CHAPTER 3

Administrators' Responsibilities Regarding Negligence

Abstract Chapter 3 explores the element of *duty* as it relates to a public school employee's responsibilities. It introduces consideration of when a duty exists and whether it is owed, as well as whether a duty has been breached and injury has occurred. Viewing negligence through the lenses of case law, history, and the public policy expectations of educators and public education, readers are helped to understand the relationships upon which liability rests. Scenarios for readers to explore help to translate the theory of Chap. 2 into administrative practice.

Keywords Duty • Safety • Roles • Reasonably Prudent Person • Public policy

Many individuals may find themselves vulnerable to liability for negligence in the context of the school environment. For the purposes of this book, our focus is on administrators and their particular charges. From that perspective, using case law and public policy, we will examine whether and how the interpretation of the elements of negligence may be evolving from what has traditionally been accepted as an administrator's potential for liability. However, before proceeding to the "what-ifs," it is important to consider what is currently accepted as administrators' responsibilities regarding negligence.

© The Author(s), under exclusive license to Springer Nature Switzerland AG 2024
B. Godett, L. M. Nobile, *Exploring Administrative Decision-Making in Public Education*,
https://doi.org/10.1007/978-3-031-58782-5_3

Overall and simply, the responsibilities of public school administrators reflect their roles as leaders of large numbers of people performing a wide variety of tasks related to the care of students. Various duties have been connected to these responsibilities. Whether a duty exists and whether it is actually owed in a certain situation can be somewhat confusing. It is referred to in the 1976 case of *Peter W. v. San Francisco Unified School District*:

> [W]hether a defendant owes the requisite 'duty of care,' in a given factual situation, presents a question of law which is to be determined by the courts alone....[J]udicial recognition of such duty in the defendant, with the consequence of his liability in negligence for its breach, is initially to be dictated or precluded by considerations of public policy. (*Peter W. v. San Francisco Unified School District*, 1976, at 822)

But the question of whether a duty exists or is owed has also been interpreted in the reverse! It's been said, "Whether a 'duty' exists is a question of law—that is, something which is decided by a court, not a jury. Deciding whether a 'duty' is owed by a defendant to a plaintiff is essentially a public policy decision" (Pringle, 2005, p. 1). It is fair to say this is a good illustration of how cases have been won and lost based upon how they have been argued.

Regardless of the interpretation, what is clear is that duty is bound by both public policy and the law. And while the law can often be construed in a manner that is concrete, public policy differs widely—meaning, liability for negligence can easily change!

Public policy, broadly stated, is the way the government (or a government agency) responds to a problem with respect to the needs of its public. Among other institutions, "government" or "public agency" includes traditional public schools. [Note: Charter schools, as they are public schools, have also been determined to be "state actors" (and, thus, considered as government or public agencies) as the Fourth Circuit decided in the recent case of *Peltier v. Charter Day School, Inc.* (2022). However, the U.S. Supreme Court in April 2023, declined to take that case on appeal, thus leaving in question the "legal status of charter schools" (Walsh, 2023).]

Public policy can be made up of laws and practices and will vary with the times and in different locations. It is heavily dependent upon facts or what legal parlance would call the "totality of the circumstances." One way of looking at public policy is to consider it an umbrella under which laws and practices fall. The public policy umbrellas most commonly associated with education largely cover the general areas of safety and the provision of learning opportunities.

A most well-known and accepted public policy associated with public education is that school, whether a physical structure or a representation of democratic ideals, has always been regarded as a safe place for growth and for learning, particularly about what it means to participate as part of our democracy. So implied *The Northwest Ordinance* in 1787 which stated, "Religion, morality, and knowledge, being necessary to good government and the happiness of mankind, schools and the means of education shall forever be encouraged" (Zeiger, n.d.).

Asking public school administrators to identify their responsibilities regarding negligence would most likely result in their mentioning safety in some way as a duty of care based on those with whom they share a special relationship. Though they wouldn't necessarily say it using those terms, their understanding would be clear. They are entrusted with keeping students and staff safe. If injury results as a consequence of breaching their duty, they could be liable for negligence.

Those involved in public education are generally responsible for their own actions. There is no assumption of responsibility for one person's negligent act on another (National School Boards Association, 2003, pp. 2–3). For example, should a teacher leave a classroom of students unattended, the *teacher* could be negligent if a fight breaks out in their absence between students known to have hostilities toward one another, and someone is injured. However, the *administrator* could be deemed negligent for failing to communicate clear expectations for teachers not to leave students unattended—even if this is something that should be assumed as common logic.

Another action administrators could take to ensure safety and protect themselves from liability in this circumstance would be to set out steps for a coverage plan should teachers unexpectedly and unavoidably need to leave the classroom. Planning is thus a key responsibility of administrators to avoid liability for negligence as will become evident in the examples shared later in this chapter.

There is no way to determine whether this definition of negligence is universally understood among administrators or those they serve. It helps to consider history, specific examples from practice, and case law resulting from judicial decisions. This is what we will strive to do in this chapter and in those that follow.

That school administrators are viewed as public servants helps to define their duties with expectations that leaders assume a flawless public image demonstrating prototypical behaviors, scholarship, wisdom, morality, and stability to which students can aspire. Even under the most challenging circumstances, the tacit assumption of this somewhat idealized persona has long identified administrators as role models. Such expectations have helped define the duty of school administrators not only as those who can keep students and staff safe, but also as those with a crucial responsibility to prepare students for future roles as productive members of their communities.

There have, likewise, been very clear-cut, traditionally defined roles for students. Probably one of the best illustrations of these traditional roles is expressed by Justice Hugo Black in his 1969 dissent in *Tinker v. Des Moines Independent Community School District* when he said, "[T]axpayers send children to school on the premise that, at their age, they need to learn, not teach" (*Tinker v. Des Moines*, 1969, at 522). In that role, according to Black, students are subject to school discipline, a duty he views school administrators as sharing with parents. From the Justice's dissent, "School discipline, like parental discipline, is an integral and important part of training our children to be good citizens—to be better citizens" (*Tinker v. Des Moines*, 1969, at 524).

Black puts students squarely in their place, saying, "I, for one, am not fully persuaded that school pupils are wise enough, even with this Court's expert help from Washington, to run the 23,390 public school systems in our 50 States" (*Tinker v. Des Moines*, 1969, at 525–526).

Parents have traditionally been supporters of that duty. They have complemented the administrator's role by providing oversight of their children's growth and development generally, but particularly at home, with school administrators and staff standing *in loco parentis*, or in place of the parents, during the school day.

While this helps to place the "reasonably prudent person" standard mentioned in Chap. 2 in the context of schools, with so many players involved in public education, through which "reasonably prudent person's" eyes does justice see? In his 1964 treatise on school personnel and negligent conduct, Reynolds Seitz, a former school administrator and law professor, explains that students fall within the category of "neighbors" and that teachers and administrators "must act toward pupils as would the reasonable, prudent person or parent under the circumstances." The public policy thus applied here is that a person "must take reasonable care to avoid acts or omissions which he can reasonably foresee would be likely to injure his neighbor" (Seitz, 1964, p. 496).

It certainly makes sense.

Awareness of these roles has helped establish and, to a certain extent, cement the special relationships between various school stakeholders. It is instructive, therefore, to explore, even briefly, some specific examples of administrators' responsibilities regarding negligence vis-à-vis these relationships. First, some questions:

- Once the relationships are established, how does an administrator know the extent of that duty?
- What are the determining factors in keeping students safe?
- Is there more than one expectation based on public policy?
- Do those expectations change based upon the history in a particular district or in schools generally and/or over time?

Let us consider some examples loosely based upon real situations in public schools. As you read, consider not only the elements of negligence outlined in Chap. 2, but also the probability or foreseeability of the risk of injury in each situation. How would each story end if the principal was guilty of negligence? Was not guilty of negligence?

Bear in mind the importance of considering public policy. Seitz notes, "[S]ometimes risk may reasonably be run with the full approval of the community" (Seitz, 1964, p. 497). Seitz goes on to note the difficulty a jury would have determining the reasonableness of a decision, advising against providing guidance for educators that puts them in a "legal strait jacket" compromising children's ability "to learn and develop responsibility" (Seitz, 1964, p. 498).

Day-to-day administrative decisions involve both risk and balance in keeping students safe and helping them develop as responsible adults. See what you think about the following examples.

Scenario #1: The Concert That Went to the Dogs

The scenario: At the end of the school day, the same day on which the school's spring concert was scheduled, a bomb threat was received at the school. All students and staff, except for some in the main office, had left for the day. The principal immediately notified the police, who arranged for bomb-sniffing dogs to comb the building. The principal and a member of her office staff who volunteered, remained in the office to place a call to every parent whose child was scheduled to perform that evening, notifying them that the concert would have to be postponed to the next evening. Once all calls had been placed, they vacated the office. The police were not pleased that the principal insisted upon remaining in the building; however, the district's technology was such that the records including all parent contact information could not easily be transported or transferred to another building to make the calls from a different location.

Think it through: When considering liability for negligence after the fact, it is sometimes a good idea to start by looking at whether or not injury occurred. In this case had injury occurred? Why might the principal have made the decision to remain in the building to personally get in touch with each parent? Could the principal have waited until the dogs finished combing the building to make his decision? Was injury foreseeable and something over which the principal had any control? Would the principal have been liable for negligence in this situation? Would your response to these questions be different if you had known that this situation took place in the days before email and the type of technology access administrators have to student databases today?

Scenario #2: Parents in Cars

The scenario: Pupil drop-off at a suburban middle school was a daily traffic nightmare for the school's principal. This neighborhood school was bordered on three sides by houses and woods and was accessible from a side street; however, it faced out onto a busy, divided four-lane town road. There was no traffic light where the side street emptied into the four-lane road, only a stop sign and a sign indicating drivers could make a right turn only.

Parents pulled up in sometimes last-minute efforts to release students from their care to walk unescorted up a short path and into the school building. Sometimes vehicles would cram the narrow street pulled up right beside one another leaving students to dart between them. Driving away found parents maneuvering their cars around others, sometimes backing up into those behind them causing damage to vehicles and, most importantly, potential injury to students. Despite the right-turn-only sign, every now and then someone attempted to turn left, sometimes cutting off the car beside them.

Most mornings the principal could be seen at the sidewalk by the curb on the side street assisting students leaving cars and entering the school. At times a police officer was present to assist with traffic flow.

The only entrance to the faculty parking lot was also off this same street parents used for drop-off. As a result, staff members sometimes arrived late if they found themselves sitting in drop-off traffic.

Think it through: Had a student been injured, would the principal have been liable for negligence? Why or why not? Who might have been? Why or why not? What could have been done differently? What was the principal's responsibility? What was the responsibility of the police or the district to assist?

Scenario #3: The Walk-Out

The scenario: One afternoon, in the middle of a school day in an urban district, the building principal and his assistant, along with a number of teachers and students, marched out of school, crossing city streets and heading to the district office in an act of protest. No prior notification was provided to the district's math supervisor, who was left behind as the remaining administrator in the high school building. He became aware of the walk-out when students came to his office, located in a hallway distant from the main office, to inform him there was no one supervising students at lunch in the cafeteria. This supervision was not normally his responsibility.

Think it through: Could the principal in this situation have been liable for negligence? Under what conditions? What about the assistant principal? The math supervisor?

Scenario #4: The Call of the Wild

The scenario: The principal of a suburban elementary school received several late-night phone calls from the school's head of maintenance to say he had been contacted by the district's security company about a possible intruder in the school. He informed the principal after each call and followed up by going into the building each night. He found nothing. After one call, the principal decided to join him to check out the building together and scope out what might be happening. Joined this time by the police, they all agreed to separate and comb the building using flashlights to light their way. Again, nothing was found to be amiss. There was no indication of a break-in. Finally, early one morning the head of maintenance arrived at school to see a huge groundhog sitting in the middle of the front lobby. He quickly called the principal who rushed to the school. The principal alerted the superintendent, and a call for assistance was also made to animal control, to no avail. Using a broom, the principal chased the groundhog to the end of the hall where it lodged under a heating unit. The head of maintenance and his staff eventually were able to coax the animal out from under the heater, and it fled to another entryway where it was exited from the building.

Think it through: What detail(s) are missing from this scenario that would better enable you to determine the principal's potential for liability? How does public policy factor into this scenario? What might the district's responsibility be? What should the follow-up be?

Scenario #5: Sexual Assault?

The scenario: A female student was found engaging in what she and a male student referred to as consensual sex in an elevator in a suburban high school building after the end of a school day. They were discovered by the district's Director of Buildings and Grounds who had come to conduct a routine inspection of the elevator. The Director reported the assault to the Principal who promptly launched an investigation of the incident and also informed the police. In addition to school consequences that were set in motion, the female student's parents pressed charges against the young man and accused the Principal of negligence in properly supervising students in the building after school hours.

Think it through: What details would help you determine negligence on the part of the principal? What would you want to know about each student and any prior relationship between them? Would having this information matter? What about the conditions of the building that might have made it easier for such an incident to have taken place?

Scenario #6: Unimagined Abuse

The scenario: Two middle school students attacked a fellow student in their grade after school hours and off school grounds, tying him to a tree and stabbing him. While the stab wounds were not life-threatening, the student required extensive hospitalization and rehabilitation to recover. Fully recovered, he was set to re-enter school; however, the two who had committed the atrocious act would also still be in attendance. The principal was legally powerless to prevent this from happening based upon a state law.

Think it through: Because the principal is unable to affect a change in the circumstances of the injured student's return, should further injury to the student occur, how could the principal potentially be deemed negligent? What options are available to the principal? What responsibility does the principal have to create a safe learning environment for the student? What steps might the principal consider putting in place?

SCENARIO #7: LET'S LUNCH!

The scenario: An elementary school principal inherited a long-standing tradition where parents were allowed to drop in unannounced to enjoy lunch with their child. This practice was regarded as important by this community where most parents worked schedules that allowed little family time after school hours. While most parents provided advance notice, not all did. During holiday times and birthdays, this practice sometimes resulted in extraordinary lunchroom chaos with deafening noise levels and a shortage of seating for some students. On various occasions there were always students whose parents did not, or could not, participate. Doors required to be locked for safety were propped open to facilitate parents' entering and leaving the building which meant that some attended without first checking in at the office per school protocol.

Think it through: What responsibility does the principal have in this situation? What complicates that responsibility? Does the complication justify the principal's accepting the status quo? Does public policy enter into this situation in any way? If so, how?

The list of situations where administrators could unintentionally or intentionally fall in harm's way is endless. "Next-gen" negligence suggests that, in addition to the more well-known experiences of school leaders, liabilities yet to be fully realized lie in wait. Thus we proceed, not intending to be cautionary, but informed, so that anticipation may yield positive results.

REFERENCES

National School Boards Association. (2003, April). Negligence: Legal pointers for public schools. In *A school law primer: Part II*. https://cdn-files.nsba.org/s3fs-public/reports/Negligence-Legal-Pointers-for-Public-Schools.pdf?DhsR

Peltier v. Charter Day School, Inc., No. 20-1001 (4th Cir. 2022).

Peter W. v. San Francisco Unified School District, 60 Cal. App. 3d 815 (1976).

Pringle, H.R. (2005, Winter). *School Law Advisory #480 Educational malpractice claims: A brief history*. SchoolLaw.com. https://schoollaw.com/wp-content/uploads/pdf/480.pdf

Seitz, R.C. (1964). Legal responsibility under tort law of school personnel and school districts as regards negligent conduct toward pupils. *Hastings Law Journal, 15*(4), 495–519. https://repository.uclawsf.edu/cgi/viewcontent.cgi?article=1793&context=hastings_law_journal

Tinker v. Des Moines Independent Community School District, 393 U.S. 503 (1969).

Walsh, M. (2023, June 26). Supreme Court declines to hear closely watched case on charter schools. *EducationWeek*. https://www.edweek.org/policy-politics/supreme-court-declines-to-hear-closely-watched-case-on-charter-schools/2023/06

Zeiger, H. (n.d.). *Educating citizens: Have we kept the founders' ideals for higher education?* Pepperdine School of Public Policy. Retrieved January 10, 2021, from https://publicpolicy.pepperdine.edu/academics/research/policy-review/2008v1/educating-citizens.htm

CHAPTER 4

Negligence and the Right to an Education

Abstract Chapter 4 is framed around the belief that administrators need to have a clear understanding of the history of public education from a legal perspective if they are to skillfully navigate the potential for professional liability and best serve their students. Explored within are themes essential to the evolution of students' rights within the context of a right to education that the U.S. Supreme Court has never deemed "fundamental." Outlined through the histories of landmark legal challenges is the struggle to identify the rights of students and parents in public education, with an emphasis on the early 1900s through to the present day. This chapter serves as an introduction to what the authors term "next-gen negligence."

Keywords Constitution • Fundamental right • U.S. Supreme Court • Responsibility • Standing • Duty

Surprising to many is that reading through the U.S. Constitution's articles and amendments reveals no reference to a right to education, public or otherwise. The closest reference is found in the Tenth Amendment which reads, "The powers not delegated to the United States by the Constitution, nor prohibited by it to the States, are reserved to the States respectively, or to the people" (U.S. Const. amend. x). Among those powers reserved to the states is the assurance of an education, which actually does appear in every state constitution (albeit with slight language differences, which we will explore in a later chapter).

There has been much debate in cases brought to the courts regarding whether education has a proper place in the U.S. Constitution and should be deemed a "fundamental" right. A fundamental right is a right so essential that, unless the government is able to show a compelling reason otherwise, it cannot be taken away from those entitled to receive it.

Examples of fundamental rights are those contained in the first ten amendments known as the Bill of Rights and include, among others, freedom of speech and of the press, freedom to assemble peacefully, freedom to practice one's religion, and the freedom not to be deprived of life, liberty, or property without due process of law. Other freedoms have been determined as fundamental by virtue of U.S. Supreme Court decisions, including, but not limited to, the right to marry and the right to vote.

Although the argument for education as a fundamental right under the U.S. Constitution has not been successful thus far, court decisions in several states have declared education to be a fundamental right for their citizens. In a recent case, *William Penn School District v. Pennsylvania Department of Education*, the Pennsylvania Commonwealth Court concluded: "the right to public education is a fundamental right explicitly and/or implicitly derived from the Pennsylvania Constitution" (*William Penn School District v. Pennsylvania Department of Education*, 2023, at 747).

The U.S. Supreme Court has danced around this issue of education as a fundamental right intentionally or unintentionally in cases over the years. In 1925 in a case known as *Pierce v. Society of Sisters*, the Court ruled that parents had discretion over *where* to educate their children. This was a case that challenged the Oregon Compulsory Education Act requiring every parent or guardian to send their child to the public school where they resided.

The Society of Sisters and co-defendant Hill Military Academy were private for-profit corporations that ran numerous facilities dedicated to educating children at all grade levels, including orphans. This case was in part about securing the future of these businesses, the Court viewing the right of these corporations to run schools as a fundamental property interest.

While in this case the Court acknowledged a state's right to regulate schools, it also recognized a parent's or guardian's right to select the education deemed best for their child as a liberty interest. So while the Court did not declare education "fundamental" under the U.S. Constitution, here, it upheld both the state law requiring that children attend school and a parent's right to choose between public education or private options.

Important to note in contrast, as we talk later about parental rights, is an earlier case in 1923, *Meyer v. Nebraska*, where the Court supported the right of the school to decide *how* students could be taught. In this case a parochial schoolteacher was said to have violated a state law forbidding the teaching of any modern language besides English to children not yet successfully passing eighth grade. The case is most interesting as one considers present-day constraints imposed by state legislatures on what can be taught in schools. In *Meyer* the Court looked at the population toward whom the law was directed, noting its violation of the liberty rights of those speaking languages other than English. The Court also refers to the case's place in history immediately following World War I and the fears that resulted in greater emphasis on patriotism.

While they speak to aspects of the right to an education, both these cases illustrate how state laws impose certain expectations on schools and educators. Violating the laws could subject educators to concerns about injury to students. With that in mind, it is significant to share the conclusion of Justice McReynolds' opinion in *Meyer* where he states,

> *It is well known that proficiency in a foreign language seldom comes to one not instructed at an early age, and experience shows that this is not injurious to the health, morals or understanding of the ordinary child.* (*Meyer v. Nebraska*, 1923, at 403)

Negligence is not mentioned, though its elements are certainly implied as having been a consideration regarding the potential for injury to students.

While *Meyer* makes mention of injury to the "ordinary child," the responsibility of a school to ensure the individual rights of a particular student did not come to the Court until 1943 in a remarkable and historical turn of judicial events.

The case of *Minersville School District v. Gobitis* in 1940 raised the question of whether students who refused to salute the flag on the basis of their religious beliefs could be forced to comply at the cost of facing expulsion from school. It is significant to note that at this point in history the United States hadn't yet committed to joining the Allies in World War II and, as with *Meyers*, there was a strong emphasis on demonstrations of national pride. The Court in an 8-1 decision supported the school over the students, ruling that states have an interest in ensuring "the binding tie of cohesive sentiment" as the "ultimate foundation of a free society" (*Minersville v. Gobitis*, 1940, at 596).

As for the students, Justice Frankfurter noted that it is one thing for the Court to say all children must attend public schools (referring to *Pierce*) and quite another to challenge the legislature's belief "that a particular program or exercise will best promote in the minds of children who attend the common schools an attachment to the institutions of their country" (*Minersville v. Gobitis*, 1940, at 599). This begs consideration of a most interesting contrast between the right to an education, which has been determined by the Court not to be a fundamental right, and rights of students while being educated, which in the case of certain rights, may be fundamental!

Justice Harlan Stone voiced the sole dissent in *Gobitis*, his words unknowingly prophesying the emergence of a focus on individual rights just a few years later. In his dissent he noted, "The guarantees of civil liberty ... presuppose the right of the individual to hold such opinions as he will and to give them reasonably free expression" (*Minersville v. Gobitis*, 1940, at 604).

By 1943 in the case of *West Virginia v. Barnette*, Justice Stone found himself among the 6-3 majority deciding a similar case but this time affirming the civil liberties of individual students. Justice Robert Houghwout Jackson, writing the opinion for the Court, noted:

> *The freedom asserted by these appellees does not bring them into collision with rights asserted by any other individual. ... Nor is there any question in this case that their behavior is peaceable and orderly. The sole conflict is between authority and rights of the individual.* (*West Virginia State Board of Education v. Barnette*, 1943, at 631)

These two cases can be viewed as a fulcrum of significant change in the Court's involvement with public education. These cautionary words of Justice Frankfurter in *Gobitis* came to life just three years after that decision:

> *It is not our province to choose among competing considerations in the subtle process of securing effective loyalty to the traditional ideals of democracy, while respecting at the same time individual idiosyncrasies among a people so diversified in racial origins and religious allegiances. So to hold would, in effect, make us the school board for the country. That authority has not been given to this Court, nor should we assume it.* (*Minersville v. Gobitis*, 1940, at 594)

Barnette tips the balance with the Court's taking a more decisive role in decisions directly regarding or strongly connected to public education, individual liberties triumphing in many judgments and enacted laws, especially toward the end of the twentieth century. These include but certainly are not limited to the decisions in *Brown v. Topeka I and II* (1954 and 1955), the Individuals with Disabilities Education Act (1975), *Tinker v. Des Moines* (1969), Section 504 of the Rehabilitation Act of 1973, the Americans with Disabilities Act and its amendments (1990 and 2008), and the Voting Rights Act (1965). Additionally, public policy was tremendously influenced over these years by the Civil Rights movement, the Women's Rights movement, and the Vietnam War.

A unanimous decision in *Wisconsin v. Yoder* introduced the idea that family values imparted through religious practice, at least in the Amish community, could be a determining factor in school attendance beyond successful completion of the eighth grade. It is important to note, however, Chief Justice Burger's opinion:

> *[C]ourts are not school boards or legislatures, and are ill-equipped to determine the "necessity" of discrete aspects of a State's program of compulsory education. This should suggest that courts must move with great circumspection in performing the sensitive and delicate task of weighing a State's legitimate social concern when faced with religious claims for exemption from generally applicable education requirements. (Wisconsin v. Yoder, 1972, at 235)*

Remember this caveat as a consideration in our chapter on free expression regarding the weight of a court's influence over administrative and district practices.

The evolution of laws since 1943 has led us to where we are today—positively impacting public education in many ways, but leaving it and educators quite vulnerable in others, especially in recent years. An administrator's responsibilities regarding negligence have evolved as a result, complicating their roles. This has led to decisions, or to a lack of decision-making, that almost leaves students in the position of anticipating their own "fundamental" rights within their particular school setting. Negligence becomes the "cause of action" relative to other laws if someone, in our case the administrator, fails to uphold those laws—a "cause of action" defined as "a set of predefined factual elements that allow for a legal remedy" (Legal Information Institute, Cause of action, n.d.-a).

Let's go back to *Gobitis* for a moment and the students who were expelled for refusing to salute the flag on the basis that doing so, in their minds and religious practice, would be akin to worshiping a graven image. Consider the following:

- Was it the duty of the administrator to compromise an individual's conscience in order to safeguard what society deemed necessary?
- Would failing to take disciplinary action in this case have been a breach of the administrator's duty to the secular interests of other students to benefit the good of all?
- Would the injury inflicted by this breach subject others to a denial of *their* freedoms based upon beliefs "dissident and ... obnoxious to the cherished beliefs—even of a majority" (*Minersville v. Gobitis*, 1940, at 594)?

When two sides possess conflicting rights, where does the administrative duty lie? The justices recognized the conundrum in this case, not minimizing the importance of the free exercise of religion under the First Amendment. In Justice Frankfurter's words, "So pervasive is the acceptance of this precious right that its scope is brought into question, as here, only when the conscience of individuals collides with the felt necessities of society" (*Minersville v. Gobitis*, 1940, at 593).

In saying this, Frankfurter actually helps define administrative responsibility toward students—that it is guided and bound, as it were, by "the felt necessities of society." And while he notes that "every possible leeway should be given to the claims of religious faith" (*Minersville v. Gobitis*, 1940, at 594), he also notes, "The mere possession of religious convictions which contradict the relevant concerns of a political society does not relieve the citizen from the discharge of political responsibilities" (*Minersville v. Gobitis*, 1940, at 595).

So the administrator, in keeping students safe, at least as established in this case, also had a duty to ensure that students conform to "political responsibilities." This is indeed a nod to the idea noted in Chap. 3 that *whether* a duty is owed may be determined by public policy.

How interesting—especially considered in terms of some most recent cases where students have accused schools of failing to provide them with education—both in literacy and in civics—such that they can properly assume their responsibilities as citizens in our democracy. Two cases in recent years particularly stand out: *Gary B. v. Whitmer* and *A.C. v. Raimondo*.

Gary B. was a case in the Sixth Circuit where Detroit public school students and parents alleged that the State of Michigan had not ensured a fundamental right to literacy for all children and that conditions under which children received their education were not at all equitable in districts across the state. The case and supporting documents describe the conditions under which these children attended school with great and horrific particularity, including inoperable toilets and drinking fountains; 25-year-old textbooks for only 6 of the 35 students in a class; students teaching where there are no teachers; and inoperable heating and air conditioning (Phillips, 2020). Further, learning conditions were subject to packed learning spaces; infestations of "mice and their droppings"; conditions so cold that "on some days students can see their breath inside their classrooms"; flooded classrooms; and books literally taped together with broken spines (Class Action Complaint, 2018, at 8, 54, 78–86).

Ultimately, the case was settled before it could be appealed to the U.S. Supreme Court with Governor Whitmer's agreeing to fund support for literacy education as well as a monetary settlement for the student plaintiffs to receive additional support for their learning. Evan Caminker, co-counsel for the case, calls the Sixth Circuit's decision in *Gary B.* "groundbreaking, being the first to recognize a right of access to literacy" (Whitmer, 2020).

It is important to consider this in terms of what it could imply for a school administrator's responsibility and potential liability for negligence.

The case of *A.C. v. Raimondo* is similar to *Gary B.* in that students filed suit on the basis that they were not provided with an education—in this case, a civics education. Students asked the First Circuit court to declare that they (and all U.S. students) have a constitutional right "'to a meaningful educational opportunity' that will adequately prepare them to be 'capable' voters and jurors, as well as to exercise all of their constitutional rights and function as 'civic participants in a democratic society'" (*A.C. v. Raimondo*, 2020, at 174–175).

What is most telling regarding both the responsibility for learning and the potential for negligence on the part of schools is the conclusion to Justice William E. Smith's opinion in this case which, again, evokes public policy. He says:

> Plaintiffs should be commended for bringing this case. It highlights a deep flaw in our national education priorities and policies. The Court cannot provide the remedy Plaintiffs seek, but in denying that relief, the Court adds its voice to Plaintiffs' in calling attention to their plea. Hopefully, others who have the power to address this need will respond appropriately. (*A.C. v. Raimondo*, 2020, at 197)

The student plaintiffs in *Raimondo* lost their case on the basis that a constitutional right to the study of civics does not exist. The question becomes one of adequacy and equity in the provision of a basic education in the state. In his opinion Justice Smith stresses the importance of respecting local control of school districts, provided that the actions of the state were not "arbitrary or irrational" (*A.C. v. Raimondo*, 2020, at 197), his words bringing us back to Justice Frankfurter's admonition in *Gobitis* that the Court must be concerned about becoming "the school board for the country," which Justice Frankfurter concluded was not the Court's role. Justice Smith places the responsibility for education on "others who have the power to address this need."

It will be interesting to see how this plays out in the future in Rhode Island, but it certainly seems to give authority to school committees and administrators—and, thus, responsibility, which could translate into the potential for liability.

It is difficult to leave this topic without mentioning a couple of important points—especially as we venture into our consideration of "next-gen" negligence and how that differs from traditional understandings of negligence. The cases discussed in this chapter have been clear about several things.

First, they illustrate a direct relationship between the school and its students with an administrative duty to uphold law, policy, and/or established procedure. In each case students had what is known as "standing" to file suit. To have standing means that "plaintiffs have sustained or will sustain direct injury or harm and that this harm is redressable" (Legal Information Institute, Standing, n.d.-b).

Second, the comments shared in the justices' opinions indicate that responsibility for different decisions rests with different actors. Certain decisions, such as those dealing with the allocation of funds within a district (*Gary B.*, 2020) and decisions about how lessons are taught (*Meyers*), are the direct responsibility of those in the schools. Schools also have some control over free expression and free exercise of religion vis-à-vis the implementation of school rules (*Gobitis* and *Barnette*). Some decisions are the responsibility of both the state and the schools such as the appropriation of state funds to districts and the development of uniform state curriculum guidelines (*Gary B.* and *A.C.*). And still other decisions are under the direct control of parents such as decisions about where students are to be educated (*Pierce*).

Thus, considering next-gen negligence, it will be important to keep certain things in mind:

- While administrators' duty has primarily been to students and to staff (in ethical and contractual terms), are there also administrative duties emerging to parents and taxpayers?
- In the case of injury, who has standing to file suit? And what constitutes injury?

REFERENCES

A.C. v. Raimondo, 494 F. Supp. 3d 170 (D.R.I. 2020).
Class Action Compl., Gary B. v. Snyder, 313 F.Supp. 3d 852, 856 (E.D. Mich. 2018) (16-CV-13292). https://clearinghouse.net/doc/83262/
Gary B. v. Whitmer, No. 2:16-cv-13292 (6th Cir. 2020).
Legal Information Institute. (n.d.-a). *Cause of action.* https://www.law.cornell.edu/wex/cause_of_action#:~:text=A%20cause%20of%20action%20is,judicial%20precedent%2C%20or%20administrative%20regulation
Legal Information Institute. (n.d.-b). *Standing.* https://www.law.cornell.edu/wex/standing
Meyer v. Nebraska, 262 U.S. 390 (1923).
Minersville School District v. Gobitis, 310 U.S. 586 (1940).
Phillips, C. (2020). A class action lawsuit for the right to a minimum education in Detroit. *Northwestern Journal of Law & Social Policy, 15*(4). https://scholarlycommons.law.northwestern.edu/cgi/viewcontent.cgi?article=1205&context=njlsp
Pierce v. Society of Sisters, 268 U.S. 510 (1925).
U.S. Const. amend. x.
West Virginia State Board of Education v. Barnette, 319 U.S. 624 (1943).
Whitmer, G. (2020, May 14). *Governor Whitmer and plaintiffs announce settlement in landmark Gary B. literacy case* [Press release]. https://www.michigan.gov/whitmer/news/press-releases/2020/05/14/governor-whitmer-and-plaintiffs-announce-settlement-in-landmark-gary-b%2D%2Dliteracy-case
William Penn School District v. Pennsylvania Department of Education, No. 587 M.D. 2014 (2023).
Wisconsin v. Yoder, 406 U.S. 205 (1972).

PART II

Introducing "Next-Gen Negligence"

CHAPTER 5

Defining "Next-Gen Negligence"

Abstract In Chap. 2 the authors discussed traditional negligence and how negligence arises in the public school setting. Now, Chap. 5 aims to refocus thinking about negligence from more traditional or expected cases, such as premises liability, bullying, and discrimination cases, to current hot topics in education law as seen in recent U.S. Supreme Court decisions and arising in school districts across the country. The authors introduce what they are calling "next-gen negligence."

Keywords Next-gen negligence • Standing • Stakeholders • Curriculum • Claims • Duty of care • Injury in fact • Causation and damages

Beginning with this chapter, we will contemplate how we may expect to see negligence claims arise in the public school setting in light of less developed areas of law. For example, how will a negligence claim play out relative to new expectations about curriculum and learning resources; to new laws about what is and isn't permissible to discuss in a school setting; to advances in technology; or to demands from those beyond the schoolhouse gates, including education advocacy groups or coalitions of concerned parents.

In order to discuss next-gen negligence, we must first define it. Next-gen negligence is "the application of a traditional negligence framework to new and ever evolving injuries in fact." We do not expect that the actual elements of the tort of negligence will change as various anticipated plaintiffs bring claims under new and emerging theories of law. However, we do suspect that the application of those prongs will morph and mold themselves to the various claims and legal theories presented in today's public school education world.

Before digging into the concept of next-gen negligence, it's important to revisit in greater detail a topic introduced in Chap. 4: *who* can bring a lawsuit as a plaintiff? Generally, in order for a plaintiff to bring a claim (whether it's a claim for negligence or not), the plaintiff must have legal standing to do so. Standing is simply defined as "the capacity of a party to bring suit in court" (Legal Information Institute, Standing, n.d.).

The U.S. Supreme Court (SCOTUS) created a three-part test for determining whether a party has standing:

1. The plaintiff must have suffered an "injury in fact," meaning that the injury is of a legally protected interest which is (a) concrete and particularized and (b) actual or imminent;
2. There must be a causal connection between the injury and the conduct brought before the court; and
3. It must be likely, rather than speculative, that a favorable decision by the court will redress the injury. (*Lujan v. Defenders of Wildlife*, 1992)

We must first consider the three prongs to determine if a plaintiff indeed has standing before considering the four prongs of negligence. Put differently, *only if* a plaintiff can show that they suffered an injury in fact, that there is a causal connection between that injury and the negligence they seek to prove to the court, and that a favorable court decision will redress the injury, can the plaintiff then move forward in attempting to prove their negligence claim. The issue of standing becomes particularly interesting when thinking about "to whom the duty of care is owed," when contemplating next-gen negligence claims.

First, let's consider who some of our next-gen negligence plaintiffs may be. COVID-19 opened up a porthole view into classrooms by allowing parents an opportunity to be physically present in Zoom classrooms. They became observers of their child's schooling to an extent they had never before experienced. Previously, their involvement in the classroom was much more limited to back-to-school nights, supervising homework assignments, and reviewing report cards. COVID-19 allowed parents an opportunity to observe teachers and students in their "natural habitats." This led to parents taking a much more active, perhaps even a different, role, in their children's education.

Some parents, now having first-hand access to lessons and classroom materials, may have developed concerns based on their own personal beliefs about what and how their child should be educated, including, but not limited to, the curriculum taught, teaching methodology, and materials used for instruction. Even now that we have largely returned to in-person public school education, parents may be hesitant to relinquish this direct access to the classroom they experienced during COVID-19. Accordingly, we explore the possibility that parents, in taking a more active role in their children's education, may surface as one class of next-gen negligence plaintiffs.

The likelihood of success parents have in bringing claims on their own behalf will turn on whether they can prove they have suffered an injury in fact. Say, for example, a family attends a conservative Christian church that does not espouse acceptance of transgender identification. This hypothetical family is made up of heterosexual parents and five children, one of whom is a fifth-grade female, Mary, who attends a public middle school. Mary's curriculum includes a library period during which she is permitted to freely browse and borrow from the school's expansive collection of books.

Mary borrows the book *I Am Jazz*, by Jazz Jennings, a well-known celebrity transgender person and activist. Mary brings the book home and, at bedtime, asks her mother to read it to her. Mary has not expressed any personal gender-identity preferences previously, but now says to her mother after reading the book, "I really like Jazz. She seems so brave." The mother brings a lawsuit against the school for negligence, alleging that they should not have had *I Am Jazz* in the library catalog and claiming that she has been injured by Mary's expressing admiration for Jazz after reading the book. Has the mother actually suffered an injury in fact such that she has standing to bring this claim? What is the injury in fact? Make arguments both for and against the mother's potential for standing.

Another potential plaintiff in next-gen negligence claims is a taxpayer who has an interest in how their tax dollars are spent. Consider, now, that Mary's next-door neighbor is a childless person who still pays taxes that are used, in part, to fund the public schools. In this scenario, let's assume that Mary again borrows *I Am Jazz* from her school library, but instead of asking her mother to read it to her during bedtime, she asks the neighbor, who is also a member of Mary's church, to read it while the neighbor cares for Mary after school one day. The neighbor takes issue with this book's being provided to school children in the tax-funded public school system because the neighbor does not support transgender rights or activism. Will the neighbor have standing to bring a claim for negligence against the school district? Why or why not? In this situation, has the neighbor suffered an injury in fact? If so, what might it be?

Yet another type of potential plaintiff in a next-gen negligence case is a student, in their own right. Sticking with our hypothetical student, Mary, let's consider her now as an 18-year-old high school student, on summer break but about to begin her senior year. Mary, raised in a conservative Christian household and taught not to be accepting of any LGBTQ+ lifestyles, has started contemplating her own sexuality and is greatly looking forward to her senior health class, where the curriculum includes lessons about social health with an emphasis on forming relationships and making decisions regarding personal growth and development.

During the summer, it comes to the attention of local community members that the senior health curriculum includes lessons about sexual orientation. Some community members attend a board meeting to express their angry feelings regarding the health curriculum, after which the lessons on LGBTQ+ lifestyles are stricken from the curriculum. Mary learns of this and wants to bring a lawsuit against the board of education for negligently removing the lessons about LGBTQ+ lifestyles and different types of families. Will Mary have standing to bring this lawsuit? Why or why not? What injury in fact has Mary suffered?

We can also anticipate teachers, themselves, as possible plaintiffs in next-gen negligence cases. Consider that Mary's senior year health teacher also takes issue with the board of education's removing the lessons about LGBTQ+ lifestyles that they had a role in developing and that has been taught for a number of years. The teacher believes it is important to expose students to all different types of lifestyles and to educate them regarding how to remain healthy, no matter a student's personal life choices. Does the health teacher have standing to bring a lawsuit against the board of education for removing these lessons from the curriculum? Has the teacher suffered an injury in fact due to their not being permitted to teach what they believe is best for students?

While next-gen negligence claims will likely not just be limited to curriculum, we expect that the overwhelming majority will tie back to curriculum in some fashion. The duties that plaintiffs may allege have been breached will likely be ones that relate to what should and should not be taught in a public school setting—cases dealing with "don't say gay" laws, book bans, abortion, slavery, critical race theory, and other curriculum topics that have already made their way into mainstream media and the court of public opinion. However, just as our hypothetical student, Mary, and her parents differed in topics they wanted the curriculum to include or exclude, we expect to see claims originating from both more conservative and more liberal plaintiffs arguing for and against what should or should not be included in public school education.

As next-gen negligence remains, at its core, still a claim for negligence, assuming that our potential plaintiff has standing to bring a claim, we must determine whether a claim exists and, if so, whether a duty has been breached. We thus anticipate next-gen negligence claims will arise out of three categories: (1) a duty to educate, broadly; (2) a duty to teach certain topics; or (3) a duty *not* to teach certain topics. Returning to each of the scenarios presented above, contemplate whether the potential plaintiff (parent, taxpayer, student, teacher/administrator) was owed a duty of care and, if so, what that duty of care would be.

Now that we have identified the potential duties under a next-gen negligence framework, we must contemplate how those duties can be breached—something likely to be decided by the courts. Just as we anticipate competing interests coming from the perspectives of different stakeholders, the differing makeup of courts across the country will largely impact whether or not that duty is breached.

Consider, for example, that Mary's senior health curriculum has lesson plans not only regarding LGBTQ+ lifestyles but also regarding various aspects of healthcare related to sexual health, pregnancy prevention, and safe sex. Mary's conservative parents, who have taught Mary and her siblings that abstinence until marriage is the only acceptable choice when it comes to sex or sexual health, may feel very strongly about not educating minors of any age about sexually transmitted diseases, pregnancy prevention, and safe sex practices.

According to the Sexuality Information and Education Council of the United States ("SIECUS"), only "29 states and the District of Columbia mandate sex education" in public schools whereas "35 states require schools to stress abstinence when sex education or HIV/STI instruction is provided" (SIECUS, n.d.). In Mississippi, for example, schools are required to teach sex education, but the curriculum is not required to be comprehensive, and it "must stress abstinence through abstinence-only or abstinence-plus instruction" (Sex Education Collaborative: Mississippi, n.d.). Furthermore, Mississippi requires an "opt-in policy" where at least one week before any lessons regarding human sexuality occur, the school must obtain permission from the students' parents or guardians permitting them to participate in the sexual education classes (Sex Education Collaborative: Mississippi, n.d.). Not surprisingly, according to the Centers for Disease Control and Prevention ("CDC"), Mississippi ranks as the state with the highest rate of STD cases as of February 2023 (Rodriguez, February 13, 2023).

So, let's again consider our hypothetical student, Mary, and now let's picture her as a 17-year-old high school student in Mississippi. Mary brings home a permission slip to participate in her school's sexual education classes, but her parents refuse to sign, and Mary is not permitted to attend the classes. Despite her parents' teachings, Mary chooses to lose her virginity to her boyfriend and gets pregnant. Does Mary have a claim against the school for negligently failing to educate her? Did the school owe Mary a duty to educate her despite its opt-in policy?

What if Mary was not in Mississippi, but instead was in Florida, which has an *opt-out* policy, allowing parents or guardians to submit a written request removing their child from sex education classes. Mary's parents wrote a request to have Mary removed from the class, and Mary was not permitted to attend the instruction despite Mary's own desire to remain in the class (Sex Education Collaborative: Florida, n.d.).

What if Mary was in California, where public schools are required to teach sex education that must be comprehensive, "culturally competent for students of all sexual orientations and gender identities," and medically accurate. And what if Mary's parents opted to take her out of the class despite Mary's own desire to participate (Sex Education Collaborative: California, n.d.).

In any of the above situations, either Mary or her parents could be a potential plaintiff, as either Mary or her parents may feel that the duty owed to them either to educate broadly or to refrain from teaching certain topics was breached, based on what the curriculum was and whether or not Mary was permitted to attend the class. This is certainly much more of a gray area than what we have seen in a traditional negligence setting. You may recall J.R. from Chap. 2 where the simple issue was whether the school was negligent in having all four physical education classes participate in the HIIT warm-up. In that example, the duty owed to the student and parent was ultimately the same: to keep students physically safe while participating in class. Now, in the world of next-gen negligence, the duty can change based on whose perspective we are contemplating. Potentially, both sides could have a viable claim.

The interesting and perhaps more difficult task will be identifying the injury in fact to determine whether there is standing and what the damages are. This analysis is important because, remember, the plaintiff will not be successful if they cannot prove with a preponderance of evidence every single element of negligence, including that they suffered damages as a result of the breach of duty—in other words, that they have a viable claim. An inability to prove these elements, though, does not stop a plaintiff from bringing a claim at all because the analysis for standing to bring a claim and success on that claim are different standards.

Finally, in next-gen negligence, just as in traditional negligence, to be successful, the plaintiff will need to prove causation and damages. Often in negligence cases, it is easiest to consider causation and damages together rather than as two separate prongs—"causationanddamages," if you will. In the world of next-gen negligence, the plaintiff (whoever they may be—parent, taxpayer, student, teacher, administrator, or someone else entirely) will need to prove that the breach of duty allegedly caused the actual damages suffered. The definition of what damages are will likely evolve under this framework.

Rather than the straightforward damages we see in traditional negligence (e.g., J.R.'s broken ankle suffered as a result of tripping during gym class), in next-gen negligence, it may be much more difficult to conceptualize the damages. Is a parent damaged by their child having different opinions than they do? By having their child's opinions change and evolve as a result of being exposed to something in school that the parent may not have taught the child at home? Is a student damaged by *not* being exposed to different lessons than those they may learn at home? Is a taxpayer damaged by school children learning things the taxpayer does not believe in or subscribe to? Is a teacher damaged by not being permitted to teach their students certain lessons including lessons they may have developed as a requirement of their profession?

If we conclude that, yes, all of these various stakeholders do indeed suffer damages based on what is or is not taught in public school, how do we place a value on these damages? Instead of compensation for damages (which is typically monetary), will we see a shift in courts ordering specific performance instead (i.e., injunctions against whatever is being taught or an insistence on what the curriculum includes and a requirement that all students take and pass those subjects)? We will explore these possibilities in greater detail in the chapters that follow under the framework of next-gen negligence.

REFERENCES

Legal Information Institute. (n.d.). *Standing*. https://www.law.cornell.edu/wex/standing

Lujan v. Defenders of Wildlife (90-1424), 504 U.S. 555 (1992).

Rodriguez, E. (2023, February 13). *These states have the highest and lowest STD rates (2023)*. innerbody. https://www.innerbody.com/std-testing/std-statistics-by-state

Sexuality Information and Education Council of the United States ("SIECUS"). (n.d.). *The SIECUS state profiles 2019/2020*. Sex Ed for Social Change. https://siecus.org/state-profiles-2019-2020/

Sex Education Collaborative: California. (n.d.). *State sex education and policy requirements at a glance*. https://sexeducationcollaborative.org/states/california

Sex Education Collaborative: Florida. (n.d.). *State sex education and policy requirements at a glance*. https://sexeducationcollaborative.org/states/florida

Sex Education Collaborative: Mississippi. (n.d.). *State sex education and policy requirements at a glance*. https://sexeducationcollaborative.org/states/mississippi

PART III

Challenges to the Status Quo

CHAPTER 6

Challenges Posed by Public Policy

Abstract Chapter 6 discusses challenges that public school employees face due to public policy—a concept that is difficult to define, especially in the context of public education. By examining key court opinions, this chapter aims to encourage readers to begin thinking about how public policy affects public education in a post-COVID-19 world.

Keywords Policy • Schooling • Data • Challenges • Funding • Curriculum • Reform

There is no shortage of information and opinion affecting education as public policy echoes an overriding theme of expectations for school administrators. This should not be surprising as we think back to the case of *Peter W.* first referenced in Chap. 3. You may remember that this case spoke to the relationship of duty to public policy.

Peter W. involved a suit brought by an 18-year-old graduate against the "[San Francisco Unified School District], its agents and employees" for "negligently and carelessly fail[ing] to provide plaintiff with adequate instruction, guidance, counseling, and/or supervision in basic academic skills such as reading and writing" (*Peter W. v. San Francisco Unified School District*, 1976, at 818). The plaintiff argued that the district failed him by not properly addressing his learning disabilities and passing him from one grade to the next. The California Court of Appeals dismissed the case.

The case outlines different types of policy issues that can factor into determining whether a duty exists that could lead to potential liability for negligence. Included among these are:

- *[t]he social utility of the activity out of which the injury arises, compared with the risks involved in its conduct;*
- *the kind of person with whom the actor is dealing;*
- *the workability of a rule of care, especially in terms of the parties' relative ability to adopt practical means of preventing injury;*
- *the relative ability of the parties to bear the financial burden of injury...;*
- *the body of statutes and judicial precedents which color the parties' relationship...;*
- *in the case of a public agency defendant, the extent of its powers, the role imposed upon it by law and the limitations imposed upon it by budget; and finally,*
- *the moral imperatives which judges share with their fellow citizens. (Peter W. v. San Francisco Unified School District, 1976, at 822)*

Additionally, the court in *Peter W.* examined the various factors that public policy adds to a consideration of whether a duty has been breached and negligence has occurred. They include:

- *foreseeability of harm to the plaintiff,*
- *the degree of certainty that the plaintiff suffered injury,*
- *the closeness of the connection between the defendant's conduct and the injury suffered,*
- *the moral blame attached to the defendant's conduct,*
- *the policy of preventing future harm,*
- *the extent of the burden to the defendant and the consequences to the community of imposing a duty to exercise care with resulting liability for breach, and*
- *the availability, cost, and prevalence of insurance for the risk involved. (Peter W. v. San Francisco Unified School District, 1976, at 823)*

Public policy becomes a challenge for school administrators because public policy, by its very nature, and as is apparent from the lists outlined in *Peter W.*, is both amorphous and fluid. It is difficult to define in a manner commonly understood by those it affects, and it is easily changed based upon time, place, and the individuals involved. Adding to the challenge for administrators is that the impact of a public policy often extends beyond the limits of their direct control, especially when influenced by political gain. Consider, for example, elections to school governing bodies at the district level and to other offices at the local and state levels. Many times people serve and influence public policy affecting education who may never have taught or been an administrative leader and have little understanding of the operation of schools.

Remember that one way to view public policy is to picture it as an umbrella, the spokes of which include the laws, court decisions, and the culture and traditions of the people to whom the policy relates. There are large all-encompassing umbrellas and small ones—ones easily destroyed by fierce winds of contention and change, and others more carefully constructed to withstand the elements. There are umbrellas still waiting to be opened, and umbrellas closed but, perhaps, not forever. Just as there is an unlimited and unique supply of umbrellas, so there exists an ever-expanding supply of public policies affecting education.

Among other things, public policy in the present day seeks to define a parent's place within the scheme of public schooling and the extent to which a parent's influence over what is taught controls. Districts have operating policies in place that apply state standards to determine what is taught. Parents have a voice in the articulation of those policies through their involvement on school governance boards and other feedback mechanisms. The distinction between the authority of schools over curriculum and what is being touted as the need to respect parents' values and beliefs in determining what is taught differs among states and localities—an umbrella of established laws, precedent, and cultural assumptions that some are struggling to hold open against fierce winds.

Public policy regarding education grapples with a common understanding of the purpose of public schooling—whom it serves and why. Options for parents to choose where and how their children are to be educated have developed in number and complexity since COVID-19 school closures. With parents and teachers struggling to maintain a degree of normalcy despite uprooted expectations of what learning could and should be, it comes as no surprise that public policy regarding public education would evolve in response.

Important questions regarding public policy and school administrators' potential liability for negligence remain:

- Now that schooling has resumed in its traditional manner of in-person delivery after COVID-19, will (or should) parents be expected to resume their traditional roles?
- Should expectations for the delivery of schooling remain the same?
- Did COVID-19 provide a missed opportunity for true education reform, and is public sentiment attempting to fill perceived gaps in both learning and the system for public education as a whole?
- In a post-COVID-19 world that seems to be looking for new paths forward without the benefit of a GPS or a true destination, is there a leadership gap in public education reflecting the inertia of a system that may already have been "not enough"?

These questions are further complicated by the affinity of the press for reporting all manner of learning loss due to COVID-19 school closures but little in the way of benefits gained or recognition of issues presented by the pivot from in-person to virtual learning. Sensationalist titles like a recent opinion piece by the editorial board of the *New York Times* which reads "The Startling Evidence on Learning Loss Is In" obscure the article's reiteration of problems facing public education long before COVID-19—among them, inequities in funding and resources, attendance (more accurately seat time), and inadequate resources to address mental health concerns (*New York Times* Editorial Board, 2023).

Using evidentiary support from the National Assessment of Educational Progress (NAEP) administered by the National Center for Education Statistics, the editorial board states:

> *The school closures that took 50 million children out of classrooms at the start of the pandemic may prove to be the most damaging disruption in the history of American education. It also set student progress in math and reading back by two decades and widened the achievement gap that separates poor and wealthy children.* (*New York Times* Editorial Board, 2023)

The article goes on to place blame squarely on "education administrators and elected officials" for not addressing gaps in education by "mobilizing the country" to prepare for the "diminished lifetime earning" that will become "a significant drag on the economy" (*New York Times* Editorial Board, 2023).

Evidence? To give perspective, when Beth's school was required for one year to participate in a NAEP assessment, she asked when she would receive feedback on her students' performance. What is not widely known about this assessment is that the answer to this question is simply, you won't. Such feedback is not provided, leaving administrators helpless to use what could be beneficial data to examine the practices and curricula in their schools. It is also helpful to understand that the national sample from which the post-COVID-19 conclusions were drawn included "14,800 9-year-olds and were compared with the results of tests taken by the same age group in early 2020, just before the pandemic took hold in the United States" (Mervosh, 2022). One has to wonder whether an apples-to-oranges analysis is the best way to draw these conclusions.

Additionally, Sarah Schwartz points out in a recent *EdWeek* article that variations in assessment design from state to state, including which subjects are tested and in what grades, make it difficult to compare scores and establish trends. She also speaks to enrollment fluctuation and the level of student participation in testing as she quotes researcher Benjamin Shear, "All of these factors make it possible that the population of students who participated in testing between 2021 and 2023 changed in such a way that skews the comparison" (Schwartz, 2023).

It is easy for the public to become distraught over what appears as fact but is often information both incomplete and not totally accurate. Thinking about this in light of the public policy considerations at the start of this chapter, it is easy to see how administrators could become vulnerable in negligence for failing their duty to students on a flawed image of what public schooling is about and the real problems it faces.

A far more accurate, informative, and useful application of data would have been for the press to report on a test that assessed the same students, comparing their scores over the intervening two COVID-19 years. The reality simply is that there is no consistent system, including not only testing but also data analysis, that would provide a nationwide picture of COVID-19's impact on education. So we resort to embellished generalizations that have little impact on the real issues facing education while creating greater vulnerability for those engaged in public schooling.

Where to begin? Both a challenge for administrators and a danger to public education in general is that in some states and in certain areas of interest, public policy and school policy are becoming entangled. Intertwining the two contributes to uncertainty regarding leadership roles and, particularly, who bears a duty and to whom it is owed. Despite *Peter W.*'s attempt to separate the two—and to distinguish the role of the courts and the role of public policy in each (see Chap. 3)—a need remains to define the line more clearly between the overall role of public policy and the overall responsibility of administrators to run their schools. The U.S. Supreme Court decision in *Bethel School District No. 403 v. Fraser*, at least as regards student speech, determined that schools do have a responsibility to encourage certain values in students. "Nothing in the Constitution prohibits the states from insisting that certain modes of expression are inappropriate and subject to sanctions. The inculcation of these values is truly the 'work of the schools'" (*Bethel School District No. 403 v. Fraser*, 1986, at 683). In recent days the idea that schools have any responsibility at all to impart a system of values has become viewed as indoctrination, an idea that has promoted public policies compromising the objective autonomy of schools to deliver structured, coherent, comprehensive curricula. **This responsibility for developing school curriculum and selecting learning resources is a public policy challenge.**

This is important when considered in light of Justice Hugo Black's dissent in another student speech case, *Tinker v. Des Moines*. Referring to the essence of schooling in light of the public policy he views as accepted at the time, he says,

> *The original idea of schools, which I do not believe is yet abandoned as worthless or out of date, was that children had not yet reached the point of experience and wisdom which enabled them to teach all of their elders. ... [O]ne may, I hope, be permitted to harbor the thought that taxpayers send children to school on the premise that, at their age, they need to learn, not teach.* (*Tinker v. Des Moines Independent Community School District*, 1969, at 522)

In *Fraser* the Court also "reaffirmed that the constitutional rights of students in public school are not automatically coextensive with the rights of adults in other settings" (*Bethel School District No. 403 v. Fraser*, 1986, at 682) and that teachers, like parents, are role models as "schools must teach by example the shared values of a civilized social order" (*Bethel School District No. 403 v. Fraser*, 1986, at 683). The sticking point that becomes challenging in today's world, especially as regards public policy, is defining whose values are those expected to be shared. **This responsibility to teach students to assume their role as members of and contributors to our democracy is another public policy challenge.**

One area where a conflict of values has become a lightning rod for controversy concerns emerging public policies regarding transgender students in public schools. It is not unusual, for example, to see stories in the press about the responsibility of schools to provide information to parents when students disclose gender identities differing from their gender assigned at birth. Requests to be referred to using particular pronouns or a different name, to use certain bathrooms or locker rooms, or to participate on certain sports teams have become the basis of legal challenges. The definition of privacy memorialized in state and federal statutes and codes identifying what schools are required to disclose about a student's well-being has become unclear and subject to challenge from parents. *The responsibility to ensure a place for learning where all are welcomed without judgment is another public policy challenge. The determination of what information is deemed confidential and under what conditions is yet another.*

Are these challenges intended to undermine the responsibility of public schools to serve *all* students—or to conform to a particular ideology in contrast to a standard of professional ethics that align with case law and entitlements valuing each individual? Are these challenges evolving from changes in societal beliefs—beliefs about gender identity, the role of the family, the agency and independence ascribed to children as they grow and mature, and the fear of losing the voice and control some groups feel they might or should have over the contours of society?

Public policy can be hard to pin down and susceptible to variation based upon time and place. A good example of this is Virginia's recently enacted *Model Policies on Ensuring Privacy, Dignity, and Respect for all Students and Parents in Virginia's Public Schools*. The policies in this 2023 document supplant the state's *2021 Model Policies* which "promoted a specific viewpoint aimed at achieving cultural and social transformation in schools" (Virginia Department of Education, 2023, p. 1). It is a good example of how public policy can become entangled with school policy.

The focus of Virginia's 2021 policy document was on transgender students and how they should be treated in Virginia's public schools. The state's Department of Education believed a policy update was needed as its predecessor "disregarded the rights of parents and ignored other legal and constitutional principles that significantly impact how schools educate students, including transgender students" (Virginia Department of Education, 2023, p. 1).

The Model Policies speak to both public policy assumptions and local school division policies and practices. Several things are striking about the apparent thinking behind the Model Policies that could potentially challenge public school administrators' responsibilities in terms of negligence and to whom they owe a duty of care.

First, of note is that the Model Policies incorporate settled case law regarding a parent's right to determine the education that best suits their child, citing landmark cases such as *Pierce v. Society of Sisters* and *Wisconsin v. Yoder*. However, the Policies' primary focus on parental rights in education rests on Virginia court decisions deeming such parental rights as *fundamental* under the Fourteenth Amendment. This is something guaranteed neither under *Pierce*, which determined parents' right to select the venue for schooling that best suits their child, even if it is not public schools, nor under *Yoder*, which affirmed parents' right to remove their child from formal public education at the end of eighth grade in accordance with a family lifestyle determined by their faith. In both of these precedential cases, the system of public education was not in question, only a parent's responsibility to make decisions best for their child.

Virginia justifies its 2023 Model Policies as U.S. constitutionally sound, citing *Troxel v. Granville*, which concluded, "[I]t cannot now be doubted that the Due Process Clause of the Fourteenth Amendment protects the fundamental right of parents to make decisions concerning the care, custody, and control of *their* children" (emphasis added) (*Troxel v. Granville*, 2000, at 66). And, in fact, certain policies included in Virginia's guidance are widely accepted across the nation—that all students have a right to learn and deserve respect from schools and that parents are assumed to be able to make decisions regarding their children.

There are nuanced "commitments" to those public policies in Virginia's guidance, however, that are articulated in a manner that could be understood as expanding parental involvement in decision-making about public school curriculum and procedures extending beyond their individual children to control over the general population. These "commitments" as stated could lead school administrators through a minefield of interpretation, especially when it comes to understanding to whom they owe a duty in their roles.

As much as can be possible, a common understanding of a public policy is crucial for its authentic implementation. While Virginia's guidance is expressed in terms of a parent's rights relative to their own child, whether this guidance becomes directive and has great potential to drive at least the short-term future of public education in that state is a question. In terms of the Model Policies' execution, Virginia, its parents, and its school administrators will need to share a common understanding of the document's intent.

So when it is stated, "Schools shall defer to parents to make the best decisions with respect to their children" (Virginia Department of Education, 2023, p. 3), with the policy further defined in terms of parents having the ultimate decision-making authority regarding the pronouns their child uses at school or gender counseling or social transition received at school, what does this mean for the school administrator? What might it mean for other school employees, such as the school nurse or guidance counselor? Is there a duty of confidentiality owed to the student? Where does that duty end and the responsibility for disclosure of information to a parent begin? Has a duty to parents been established? Does the reference in the Model Policies to Code of Virginia §1-240.1 providing that a "'parent has a fundamental right to make decisions concerning the upbringing, education, and care of the parent's child'" establish a duty to parents to be met by school administrators (Virginia Department of Education, 2023, p. 2)?

And how far does that duty extend? Do parents then have a right to determine curriculum decisions regarding health, sex education, and even basic biology courses? The Model Policies go on to say, "Schools shall serve the needs of all students" (Virginia Department of Education, 2023, p. 3). The guidance here clarifies that:

Each student's individual needs should be taken into consideration by his or her school, and divisions should develop policies that encourage schools to account for these individual needs, with due sensitivity to the needs of other students and the practical requirements of the teaching and learning environment. Schools should attempt to accommodate students with distinctive needs, including transgender students. (Virginia Department of Education, 2023, p. 3)

This policy guidance seems to place control over curriculum and procedures in the hands of administrators by referencing "the practical requirements of the teaching and learning environment." However, as noted, it is difficult for administrators to be certain as to whom they owe a duty and the extent of that duty. The press release for the 2023 Model Policies states:

After the 2021 Model Policies purposefully kept parents in the dark about their child's health and wellbeing at school, the 2023 Model Policies restore parental rights in decision making about their child's identity while protecting the safety and dignity of all students. (Virginia Department of Education, Press release, 2023)

This is not to minimize the intent of the Model Policies to ensure the needs of all students are met, and to do so in a manner that bravely and clearly includes the needs of transgender students to be honored and respected. However, reading further into the section on policy development, while it is noted that the 2023 Model Policies comply with the First Amendment, it is difficult not to grasp the impact of the statement, "Many Virginians reject [the] belief" that "gender is a matter of personal choice or subjective experience, not sex" (Virginia Department of Education, 2023, p. 5). Despite that guidance in the Model Policies reassures that the needs of all students will be met and bullying will not be tolerated, are school administrators now thrust into ensuring the needs and safety of not only students, but also parents who may claim offense based upon their personal beliefs regarding sex and gender?

Notable sources have published lists of what they feel are the most pressing issues facing public education today. Among other things, they note battles over books and concerned interest in artificial intelligence (AI) (Lonas, 2023), protecting the rights of LGBTQ students, and parental control over the curriculum (Langreo, 2023). The lists converge in many places and, overall, they provide an excellent focus on what are, perhaps, the most salient public policy issues concerning the responsibilities of administrators. Looking through a public schooling lens, in general, the issues concern "provid[ing] students with the most effective teaching possible" (7 Education Policy Issues that Need to be Solved in 2020, 2020) and fulfilling "the promise of a quality education for each and every child" (Darling-Hammond, 2022). It is clear, though, that in a politically charged period in history, perspectives on the duties of school administrators in meeting these goals, indeed on the duties of public school personnel in general, may vary greatly.

From these lists and considering the public policy issues and factors from *Peter W.*, challenges to administrators based upon public policy can be derived. Some key issues such as childcare and universal preschool and the increasing prevalence of charter schools and alternatives to public education involve decisions beyond the control of school administrators and, thus, do not pose potential liability for negligence.

The following are key education policy issues and the public policy challenges they may present for school administrators in terms of negligence (in no special order of importance) (see Table 6.1):

Administrators likely face the greatest potential for being accused of negligence based upon public policy challenges. Public policy is truly in

Table 6.1 Key policy issues and corresponding levels of liability

Education issues stated as public policies	Potential liability for negligence
Funding—public policy: local, state, and federal funding is available to provide education to meet students' needs	Funding is largely inadequate across the country—and is distributed such that educational opportunities are uneven, especially affecting marginalized populations by virtue of common law, statute, and many other factors. Administrators do have responsibility to set budgetary priorities **Moderate level of control—Moderate to low liability**
Education reform—public policy: COVID-19 provided an opportunity to do schooling differently, but children's needs were not met by alternative approaches to schooling	Systemic inertia combined with a lack of time, training, and resources have created the perception that student learning, at least in the traditional sense of what has been measured, has suffered—and that administrators need to fix the problem. Depending upon the specific concern, administrators are responsible for leading, which includes assessing the organization's needs and participating in reform efforts. Whether this could result in negligence would depend upon the particular reform needed **Moderate level of control—Moderate liability**
Teacher retention—public policy: teachers will provide effective instruction to meet students' needs	Administrators are responsible for consistently following hiring protocols, as well as ensuring proper supervision takes place and professional development is provided both to support and to expand staff needs **High level of control—High liability**
Safe and sustaining school cultures and learning environments—public policy: schools are places where all students are nurtured and supported and where all who enter feel safe physically, socially, and emotionally	Administrators are responsible for following safety protocols, including communicating them effectively to staff, students, and the community. Administrators also are responsible for creating a school culture based on trust and ensuring that students are valued for who they are, not facing discrimination, bullying, or harassment **High level of control—High liability**
Curriculum changes including book bans and parents' desire to have more control over what students learn—public policy: parents should have greater say in what students learn	This is difficult to view in terms of negligence—except that administrators must follow the law. When the law conflicts with the administrator's sense of professional ethics, decisions must be made, generally not by the administrator or by the administrator alone. As such, liability for negligence here is more closely related to following state and district law and policy than it is to a duty owed to students **Low level of control—Moderate liability**

(*continued*)

Table 6.1 (continued)

Education issues stated as public policies	Potential liability for negligence
Integration of racial justice and diversity into the school culture—public policy: the school is run in a manner that reflects respect for all students and a commitment to diversity in all aspects of school life	The school administrator is key to ensuring a culture where diversity is valued and where equity is achieved to the fullest extent possible, even if it is an ongoing pursuit. Opportunities for inclusion are not only afforded in a wide variety of educational settings but fostered among all members of the school community **High level of control—High liability**
Curriculum that prepares students for the future to include workforce readiness, climate change, and AI—public policy: curriculum is developed and implemented consistent with the demands of a changing world	School districts, not particularly administrators, have been taken to task for not providing certain curricula or adequately addressing certain subject areas. The development of curriculum is not an area necessarily controlled by school administrators but rather derives from a district policy-driven process for its construction and approval for implementation **Moderate level of control—Low liability**

motion all the time—and as it is not commonly understood by all, it can be widely left up to interpretation. This doesn't mean, however, that administrators will always, or even often, be found liable.

Most important is that administrators fully understand the elements of negligence. They need to know to anticipate different types of injury. They need to recognize procedures that leave them and their school staff vulnerable. They need to have procedures in place to address any shortfalls, including providing professional development for staff. And they need to be aware of and compliant with changes to federal and state laws, as well as the most current and best practices they can implement to avoid unnecessary controversies while meeting the needs of the students they serve.

REFERENCES

7 education policy issues that need to be solved in 2020. (2020). *American University School of Education Online.* https://soeonline.american.edu/blog/education-policy-issues-in-2020/

Bethel School District No. 403 v. Fraser, 478 U.S. 675 (1986).

Darling-Hammond, L. (2022, May 2). Possible futures: The policy changes we need to get there. *Kappan.* https://kappanonline.org/possible-futures-policy-changes-darling-hammond/

Langreo, L. (2023, January 18). 5 big challenges for schools in 2023. *Education Week.* https://www.edweek.org/leadership/5-big-challenges-for-schools-in-2023/2023/01

Lonas, Lexi. (2023, August 2). *Here are the top education issues to watch going into the new school year.* The Hill. https://thehill.com/homenews/education/4131603-here-are-the-top-education-issues-to-watch-going-into-the-new-school-year/

Mervosh, S. (2022, September 1). The pandemic erased two decades of progress in math and reading. *The New York Times.* https://www.nytimes.com/2022/09/01/us/national-test-scores-math-reading-pandemic.html

New York Times Editorial Board. (2023, November 18). The startling evidence on learning loss is in. *The New York Times.* https://www.nytimes.com/2023/11/18/opinion/pandemic-school-learning-loss.html

Peter W. v. San Francisco Unified School District, 60 Cal. App. 3d 815 (1976).

Schwartz, S. (2023, November 1). What the latest student test results reveal: 5 things to know. *Education Week.* https://www.edweek.org/leadership/what-the-latest-student-test-results-reveal-5-things-to-know/2023/10

Tinker v. Des Moines Independent Community School District, 393 U.S. 503 (1969).

Troxel v. Granville, 530 U.S. 57 (2000).

Virginia Department of Education. (2023, July 18). *Model policies on ensuring privacy, dignity, and respect for all students and parents in Virginia's public schools.* https://www.doe.virginia.gov/home/showpublisheddocument/46509/638252918535370000

CHAPTER 7

Challenges Posed by Parents

Abstract Chapter 7 discusses challenges that public school employees face from one of the most important education stakeholders—parents. In recent years, parents have seemingly taken a much more active role in their children's education, whether it be in the form of voicing opinions over curriculum and library books or as advocates for their students. Teachers and administrators alike will often find themselves collaborating with parents for the good of their students. This chapter explores anticipated challenges from parents and asks readers to contemplate the duties owed by administrators, teachers, and other public school employees.

Keywords Parents • Roles • Influence • Funding • Public • State constitutions • Homeschooling

Whether you've been a parent, an educator, or a student, you are well aware of the powerful, positive force parents are in the world of public education. Traditional roles for parents have included serving on school boards or school committees and speaking before those groups; joining PTO/PTA or other similar organizations; serving as classroom, sports or music parents; taking part on various committees; voting for school budgets; and supporting their own children as members of teams convened to develop needed accommodations for learning.

Parents have taken part in planning post-prom events and class celebrations, chaperoning field trips, serving as library volunteers, and providing support to office staff and teachers. Administrators can often be seen inviting parents to coffees and soliciting their feedback in the development of school programs and events. In many districts parents have additionally been responsible for creating foundations to augment funding for special projects that would otherwise not find their way into tight budgets.

Parents have always had a significant role in the governance of schools. It would be accurate to say that the administration runs the schools and the elected (or, in some cases, appointed) school board or school committee, composed of parents and other community members, is tasked with seeing that the schools are well run.

Regardless of their role, it is important to note that parents have consistently been in position to offer support—support for the administration and teachers in school programs and activities, and support for *all* students. So what changed to bring us to "parents' rights" bills potentially placing parents in a more adversarial role toward public education and educators? These include state and federal legislation passed and pending, among them H.R. 5-Parents Bill of Rights Act, as of this writing passed only by the U.S. House of Representatives in March 2023. And how do these bills impact a school administrator's decision-making with regard to the potential for liability related to negligence?

Think back to Chap. 3 and the case of *Peter W.* which spoke to the issue of whether a duty exists and whether it is owed. Keeping this in mind, it is important to consider that, as of March 2023, Future*Ed*, a think tank out of Georgetown University's McCourt School of Public Policy which tracks Parent-Rights bills across the states, reports that

> *62 parental-rights bills in 24 states ... have been introduced or pre-filed .... Last year, 85 bills were introduced in 26 states. Six bills were signed into law-- two in Florida, two in Arizona and one in Georgia and Louisiana.* (DiMarco, 2023)

Are these bills a sign that courts may be establishing a new duty with which school administrators must comply? A duty to parents? After all, these laws are dedicated to empowering parents in ways that influence school culture and procedures that extend far beyond parents' traditional roles. The laws allow parents to assert "greater influence over their children's education that includes using public funds to send their children to private schools" (DiMarco, 2023). The level of control expected by parents includes approving curriculum, materials, and staff training, opting out when they disagree with what is being taught, and engaging the school's cooperation regarding reporting any knowledge of their child's preference for a gender identity different from that assigned at birth. Of concern is how a parent's influence over *their* children's education can end up impacting *all* children's education.

Of course, there are aspects of these pieces of legislation that fit with more traditional parental expectations for their roles relative to their child's education—expectations that many school administrators would agree are already being met. These include parents' "right to make decisions regarding their children, ... access to their child's health and education records, ... [the ability] to inquire about issues at school, ... [and the right to] be involved in and informed about their child's education." Additionally, DiMarco notes that in some states parents' rights bills include receiving "nutritional information about school meals, ... timely notification about their child's health and well-being, ... [knowledge of] all threats to the child's safety" as well as the ability to sit in on their child's class (DiMarco, 2023). Again, this is information many districts already provide.

It is easy to see how school administrators could find themselves potentially accused of negligence regarding the provisions outlined in these bills—at a cost of being placed on leave from their jobs, facing fines, or worse. Whether and (more likely when) these bills are challenged may result in courts establishing that a duty to parents in public education *exists*. Again, thinking back to the case of *Peter W.*, determining whether that duty is *owed* in a given situation, however, would likely be determined by public policy.

The word "public" is very much a part of this conversation, so it helps to understand what the word means and, especially, how it fits with education. Whom does public education serve, and is it reasonable for parents to challenge education available to all with demands for programs and procedures that align with their own personal ideologies? Do these pending or enacted state laws and proposed federal legislation create a next-gen negligence minefield for school administrators who cannot be everything to everyone without inevitably stepping on the rights of many?

According to the *Cambridge Dictionary*, the word "public" means "relating to or involving people in general, rather than being limited to a particular group of people ... involving or provided by the government, usually for the use of anyone ... [and] supported by government funds ... sometimes also by money given by private citizens" (Cambridge Dictionary, n.d.). With this understanding, when public schooling deviates from its focus on the "general" to the "particular," one might argue it departs from the spirit of this classification—or does it?

As we mentioned in Chap. 4, the Tenth Amendment of the U.S. Constitution, granting those powers not delegated to the federal government to the states, places schooling directly under the control of state constitutions and statutes. While one would think this assures education for all public school-aged children, in many cases the definition of "public school" in these constitutions and statutes is stated only in terms of funding, facilities, and governance (Zinth, 2005).

Mark Lieberman in *Education Week* echoes this connection between funding and defining public schools. He laments the apparent diversion of public monies away from what he calls "the greatest education needs of the public school system," which he references as infrastructure, accommodating the learning needs of diverse student groups, to "private schools or to parents for private decisionmaking on the educational options they choose for their children" (Lieberman, 2023).

So does "public" simply mean funding? In a sense that would be accurate as most of the budget for public schooling comes from tax dollars—tax dollars that these emerging pieces of parents' rights legislations indicate are at stake in the interests of school choice.

A more specific look into state constitutions and legislation is revealing regarding who is included among the "public" in public schools (see Table 7.1). While all states guarantee some level of education, that it is available to *all* may be implied, but not uniformly stated. The following information, provided by the Education Law Center in 2011 and accurate (with the exception of Alabama, as noted) as of 2024, shows which state constitutions and/or statutes specifically denote education for *all* either using that word or language sending a similar message:

Keeping these constitutions and legislation in mind, what does education for *all* mean? Some states clarify with words assuring equal protection for some groups that might be marginalized by virtue of race, creed, or sex, for example. However, do challenges from parents risk that some students will be denied a public education because their religious or otherwise personal beliefs do not fit with the dominant parent voices in the community? Are some children disadvantaged because funding is diverted from public school budgets for attendance at private or faith-based schools? Who monitors the shifting that results from parents' rights so

Table 7.1 A sampling of constitutional guarantees of education by state

State	Guarantee
Alabama	Education for children ages 7–21; "[s]eparate schools shall be provided for white and colored children and no child of either race shall be permitted to attend a school of the other race"[a]
Alaska	Education for all children
Arizona	Legislature providing a "general and uniform public school system" indicating what types of schools are included in this system
Colorado	"[A]ll residents of the state, between the ages of six and twenty-one years" no "distinction or classification of pupils be made on account of race or color"
Delaware	"The General Assembly ... may require by law that every child, not physically or mentally disabled, shall attend the public school, unless educated by other means"
Florida	Provides for the education of "all children residing within its borders"
Georgia	"[P]ublic education for the citizens prior to the college or postsecondary level"
Illinois	"A fundamental goal ... is the educational development of all persons ..."
Indiana	"[A] general and uniform system of Common Schools ... equally open to all"
Louisiana	"The legislature shall provide for the education of the people of the state ..."
Massachusetts	"Wisdom, and knowledge, as well as virtue, diffused generally among the body of the people ..."
Michigan	"Every school district shall provide for the education of its pupils without discrimination as to religion, creed, race, color or national origin"
Missouri	"[T]he general assembly shall establish and maintain free public schools for the gratuitous instruction of all persons in this state within ages and not in excess of twenty-one years ..."
Montana	"[T]he goal of the people to establish a system of education which will develop the full educational potential of each person"
Nebraska	"[A]ll persons between the ages of five and twenty-one years"
New Jersey	"[I]nstruction of all the children in the State between the ages of five and eighteen years"
New Mexico	"[O]pen to, all the children of school age in the state"
New York	"[A] system of free common schools, wherein all the children of this state may be educated"
North Carolina	"[E]qual opportunities shall be provided for all students"

(*continued*)

Table 7.1 (continued)

State	Guarantee
North Dakota	"[P]ublic schools which shall be open to all children of the state of North Dakota … free public schools throughout the state beginning with the primary and extending through all grades up to an including schools of higher education"
Oklahoma	"[F]ree public schools wherein all the children of the State may be educated"
South Carolina	"[F]ree public schools open to all children in the State"
South Dakota	"[A] general and uniform system of public schools … equally open to all"
Utah	"[P]ublic education system, which shall be open to all children of the state"
Virginia	"[F]ree public elementary and secondary schools for all children of school age throughout the Commonwealth"
Washington	"[M]ake ample provision for the education of all children residing within its borders, without distinction or preference on account of race, color, caste, or sex"

[a] This language from 2011 was accurate up until 2020. Noting that the Alabama constitution has been amended many, many times over the past century, the Equal Justice Initiative reported in November 2020 that the Alabama constitution had just been amended yet again to delete the racist language (Equal Justice Initiative, 2020). Short of learning that a new state constitution was proposed in 2022, it has been difficult to obtain the exact wording for an updated guarantee of education

Hunter (2011)

that they do not overwhelm the authority of those educated and experienced to run schools equitably for *all*?

What makes a public school "public" has defied definition since the concept of public education was first introduced. Even then, Boston Latin School, established as the first public school in 1635, hardly served *all* students. It took 250 years to see the first African American student to graduate in 1877 and another hundred years for the school to admit the first women in 1972 (Boston Latin School, n.d.). Even today the school operates as an "exam school" affording admission to a selective public.

When considering the wide range of student groups who, since the 1600s, were excluded from formal public schooling—those of different races, those with disabilities, those coming from other countries, and those speaking languages other than English, among others—expectations by parents that public schools be tailored to meet the needs of *their* children and *their* ideologies may not be surprising. Given the confluence of funding and opportunity, augmented by the increasing presence of vouchers for school choice, it is also not surprising that parents expect private school treatment from public school employees with an emphasis on their individual child over the needs of others.

Reality is that, based upon *Pierce* and *Meyers*, Supreme Court cases identified in Chap. 4, as well as other more recent cases such as *Wisconsin v. Yoder*, which in 1972 gave Amish parents the right to remove their children from formal education after the eighth grade, parents do have the ultimate authority over where and how their children will be educated. They even have the right to educate their children at home.

Some across the nation have chosen from among private and faith-based schools and homeschooling options for their children. Homeschooling perhaps provides parents the greatest amount of control over curriculum, even though there are still some guidelines that must be followed depending upon one's residence.

Homeschool.com is a website that shares specific information about the requirements for homeschooling in each state, those requirements varying to a certain degree. Contained on that site is information about compulsory attendance, testing, required subjects, and other prerequisites that include documentation the state needs to register a child as being "homeschooled." Requirements range from the very specific, with states including the number of hours of instruction in specific subject areas and/or an exhaustive list of subjects that must be taught, to states listing no required subjects to be taught or, in the case of Oklahoma, no actual law governing homeschooling but a provision for doing so under the state's compulsory attendance laws (Homeschool.com, n.d.).

Conservative parents and legislators have, for many years, proposed that a constitutional amendment secure parents' rights. So far they have not been successful. Mark Walsh in *Education Week* quotes Supreme Court Justice Antonin Scalia as having "suggested parents' right to control their children's upbringing was an 'unenumerated right' that was not the province of the judiciary to enforce … a right 'simply not in the Constitution'" (Walsh, 2022).

While challenges from parents may all boil down to one's perspective, parents do not have authority over where and how someone *else's* children will be educated. This is where groups such as Moms for Liberty, which have led the charge for statutes guaranteeing parental rights, have aroused the attention and the ire of many across the nation.

The challenges brought under these statutes are those that are most problematic for school leaders. For while administrators are focused on meeting the needs of students and staff, legislation such as "Parental Rights in Education," commonly known as the "Don't Say Gay" bill that passed in Florida, have become a tremendous distraction for leaders who are under tremendous pressure to conform to legislation that may violate their professional ethics and duty to their students.

Suzanne Nossel of PEN America provides the best epithet for the issue of parent challenges:

> *There is no question that parents deserve a say in shaping their children's educations; they have moral and legal responsibility for their children, and the freedom to make fundamental decisions for their families. But the rallying cry of "parents' rights" is being wielded to do far more than give parents their rightful voice. It is turning public schools into political battlegrounds, fracturing communities, and diverting time and energy away from teaching and learning.* (Nossel, September 20, 2022)

Her words are an apt conclusion to this section of our book. They echo challenges public education has received from what has been, for many years, understood as the status quo regarding stakeholder roles and responsibilities.

References

Boston Latin School. (n.d.). *BLS history*. Retrieved September 4, 2023 from https://www.bls.org/apps/pages/index.jsp?uREC_ID=206116&type=d

Cambridge Dictionary. (n.d.). *Public*. https://dictionary.cambridge.org/dictionary/english/public#

DiMarco, B. (2023, March 16). *Legislative tracker: 2023 parent-rights bills in the states*. FutureEd. https://www.future-ed.org/legislative-tracker-2023-parent-rights-bills-in-the-states/#:~:text=FutureEd%20has%20identified%2062%20parental,one%20in%20Georgia%20and%20Louisiana

Equal Justice Initiative. (November 4, 2020). *Alabama voters pass amendment 4 to address constitution's legacy of racial injustice*. Retrieved July 14, 2024 from https://eji.org/news/amendment-4-addresses-alabama-constitutions-legacy-of-racial-injustice/

Homeschool.com. (n.d.). *State homeschooling laws*. Retrieved September 5, 2023 from https://www.homeschool.com/articles/state-homeschooling-laws/

Hunter, M. (2011, January). State constitution education clause language. *Education Justice*. Retrieved September 4, 2023, from https://edlawcenter.org/assets/files/pdfs/State%20Constitution%20Education%20Clause%20Language.pdf

Lieberman, M. (2023, August 31). What does it actually mean for schools to be public? *Education Week Special Report.* https://www.edweek.org/leadership/what-does-it-actually-mean-for-schools-to-be-public/2023/08

Nossel, S. (2022, September 20). Parents should have a voice in their kids' education but we've gone too far. *Time.* https://time.com/6215119/parents-rights-education-gone-too-far/

Parents Bill of Rights Act, H.R. 5, 118th Cong. (2023–2024). https://www.congress.gov/bill/118th-congress/house-bill/5/text

Walsh, M. (2022, October 20). What do 'parents' rights' mean legally for schools, anyway? *Education Week.* https://www.edweek.org/policy-politics/what-do-parents-rights-mean-legally-for-schools-anyway/2022/10#:~:text=Debbie%20Lesko%2C%20R%2DAriz.,or%20home%20schools%2C%20and%20"the

Zinth, K. (2005, September). *What is a public school? Examples of definitions* [Data set]. ECS State Notes: State Comparisons/Statistics. Education Commission of the States. https://www.ecs.org/clearinghouse/64/13/6413.pdf

PART IV

Next-Gen Negligence in Context

CHAPTER 8

Next-Gen Negligence and Free Expression

Abstract Chapter 8 examines a familiar topic in public school law: free speech in the context of next-gen negligence. The authors discuss landmark First Amendment cases and encourage readers to think about how these seemingly well-settled concepts may play out in a modern public school district. They challenge readers to think about how the element of injury may evolve as it relates to First Amendment issues seen through a next-gen negligence lens.

Keywords First amendment • Free speech • Free expression • Student speech • Book bans • State action • Injury • Learning resources • Curriculum • Religion

As regards next-gen negligence and the First Amendment, it is perhaps best to consider free expression in terms of "that was then; this is now," which, in many cases, perhaps surprisingly, is actually "that was then; that is *still* now." Despite the proliferation of "don't say gay" laws, book bans, and politicized curriculum revisions, case law that has guided school administrators in staying safe with the First Amendment since the 1960s is still good law. Let's take a look to see how these laws comport with the challenges and potential liability administrators face today.

It is helpful to look at the text of the First Amendment to be reminded of the full extent of this fundamental right in the context of an administrator's responsibilities:

Congress shall make no law respecting an establishment of religion, or prohibiting the free exercise thereof; or abridging the freedom of speech, or of the press; or the right of the people peaceably to assemble, and to petition the Government for a redress of grievances. (U.S. Const. amend. I)

While there is already so much here for administrators to bear in mind in terms of their duties and potential breach, next-gen negligence has complicated things in recent years requiring administrators to be very much more aware of both new legislation passed in certain states and the perspectives of parents and some community groups that, up to this point in time, have not commanded as much influence as they appear to do today. While administrators may not be viewed as owing a specific duty to parent and community groups, there are times when loud voices intend to make assumptions, or are perceived as making assumptions, about a duty owed and potentially breached. This is why it is extremely important for administrators to ensure they are both following the law and fulfilling the specific responsibilities outlined in their job descriptions.

Several key cases help define the First Amendment rights of students and staff in public education. It may be somewhat comforting to be reminded of these familiar case laws pertaining to free expression that still guides administrative practice. We list them here with their key take-aways and considerations in the context of recent societal challenges.

- In 1969 a 7-2 Court in *Tinker v. Des Moines Independent Community School District* ruled in favor of students suspended after wearing black armbands to school to protest the Vietnam War. The case is perhaps best known for its words, "It can hardly be argued that either students or teachers shed their constitutional rights to freedom of speech or expression at the schoolhouse gate" (*Tinker v. Des Moines Independent Community School District*, 1969, at 506). Though subsequent cases, including those regarding social media, have attempted to define that schoolhouse perimeter, Justice Abraham Fortas clearly states in *Tinker*, "[W]e do not confine the permissible exercise of First Amendment rights to a telephone booth or the four corners of a pamphlet, or to supervised and ordained discussion in a school classroom" (*Tinker v. Des Moines Independent*

Community School District, 1969, at 513). What we take from this case is the "Tinker test":

[C]onduct by the student, in class or out of it, which for any reason—whether it stems from time, place, or type of behavior—materially disrupts classwork or involves substantial disorder or invasion of the rights of others is, of course, not immunized by the constitutional guarantee of freedom of speech. (Justice Fortas in *Tinker*, quoting *Blackwell v. Issaquena County Board of Education*). (*Tinker v. Des Moines Independent Community School District*, 1969, at 513)

- Almost 20 years later, the case of *Bethel School District No. 403 v. Fraser* resulted after a high school student delivered, at a school assembly, what the administration deemed was an inappropriate speech supporting his friend in a student council election. In this case the Court ruled 7-2 in favor of the school, distinguishing between students' political speech in *Tinker* and Fraser's speech that they viewed as "offensively lewd and indecent" (*Bethel School District No. 403 v. Fraser*, 1986, at 676). Several important points come from this case that are helpful to administrators. From Chief Justice Warren E. Berger's opinion:

*The undoubted freedom to advocate unpopular and controversial views in schools and classrooms must be balanced against the society's countervailing interest in **teaching students the boundaries of socially appropriate behavior.** Even the most heated political discourse in a democratic society requires consideration for the personal sensibilities of the other participants and audiences* (emphasis added) (*Bethel School District No. 403 v. Fraser*, 1986, at 681)

Berger goes on to identify the responsibility of the school, saying:

*The 'fundamental values necessary to the maintenance of a democratic political system' disfavor the use of terms of debate highly offensive or highly threatening to others. Nothing in the Constitution prohibits the states from insisting that certain modes of expression are inappropriate and subject to sanctions. The inculcation of these values is truly the 'work of the schools.'... **The determination of what manner of speech in the classroom or in school assembly is inappropriate properly rests with the school board.*** (emphasis added) (*Bethel School District No. 403 v. Fraser*, 1986, at 683)

- Following a little more than 20 years after *Fraser* was *Morse v. Frederick*, a case involving a student who sought and obtained his few minutes of fame when, as part of a school group anxiously waiting to see the Olympic torch run past in Juneau, Alaska, in 2002, he unfurled a sign for all to see, students and TV cameras alike: "Bong Hits 4 Jesus." He was suspended, his suspension upheld in a 5-4 Court decision on the basis that the message displayed appeared to promote illegal drug use, and the students, despite their presence outside the actual schoolhouse, were there to see the torch pass as a social event under the auspices of the school. In his opinion, Chief Justice Roberts draws two conclusions:

  1. Quoting from *Fraser*, "that 'the constitutional rights of students in public school are not automatically coextensive with the rights of adults in other settings'" and
  2. that, referring also to *Fraser*, "the mode of analysis set forth in *Tinker* is not absolute ... [as the Court in *Fraser*] certainly did not conduct the 'substantial disruption' analysis prescribed by *Tinker*" (*Morse v. Frederick*, 2007, at Section IV).

  Morse thus provides authority for schools to limit student speech when that speech has the effect of condoning or promoting illegal drug use. In Roberts' opinion,

  > *School principals have a difficult job, and a vitally important one. When Frederick suddenly and unexpectedly unfurled his banner, Morse had to decide to act—or not act—on the spot. It was reasonable for her to conclude that the banner promoted illegal drug use—in violation of established school policy—and that failing to act would send a powerful message to the students in her charge, including Frederick, about how serious the school was about the dangers of illegal drug use. The First Amendment does not require schools to tolerate at school events student expression that contributes to those dangers. (Morse v. Frederick, 2007, at Section IV)*

- Fast-forward another 20+ years, and the Court issued its decision in the case of *Mahanoy Area School District v. B.L.* This was the first time the U.S. Supreme Court weighed in on student speech in the social media context, something the lower courts had been addressing for years prior to that. In this case a high school student, failing to make her school's varsity cheerleading team, lashed out against the school and team using lewd language and gestures to her friends on Snapchat. She was suspended from the cheerleading team for the following year (*Mahanoy Area School District v. B.L.*, 2021). Unlike in *Morse*, *Fraser*, and *Tinker*, in *Mahanoy*, Justice Stephen Breyer, recognizing the omnipresent nature of social media and the periphery of the schoolhouse gates defined here by cyberspace, provided only somewhat vague guidelines for school administrators. He speaks of not setting forth in the Court's opinion "a broad, highly general First Amendment rule stating just what counts as 'off campus' speech" (*Mahanoy Area School District v. B.L.*, 2021). Rather, he notes that schools rarely assume the *in loco parentis* role of standing in for a student's parents when it comes to off-campus speech. He also speaks to the difficulty of regulating off-campus speech when it can occur 24/7—"doing so may mean the student cannot engage in that kind of speech at all." And, finally, as "America's public schools are the nurseries of democracy," "the school itself has an interest in protecting a student's unpopular expression, especially when the expression takes place off campus" (*Mahanoy Area School District v. B.L.*, 2021).

It is important to consider these cases in the context of state action to ban books and legislate curricula that have been argued to prevent students from using what educators know as higher-order skills including critical thinking and analysis in favor of the acquisition of merely basic knowledge learning only facts, dates, and data (Alvarez, 2023). These actions by states across the nation effectively remove educators from what they have been trained to do—which the Court has told us includes:

- instruction in socially appropriate behaviors (*Fraser*);
- creating in students concern for events in the world around them which can include their ability to engage in political speech (*Tinker*);
- setting boundaries for expression that run afoul of the law (*Morse*); and
- promoting tolerance for expression that may be unpopular or make people feel uncomfortable (*Mahanoy*).

Administrators' duty to uphold these legal precedents translates into their duty to support teachers in determining appropriate pedagogy and resources for their students, as well as their duty to ensure students receive the opportunities to learn enshrined in their state's constitution. With this in mind, the Court clearly states that people should be respected for their "personal sensibilities" and should not have to endure speech that is "highly offensive or highly threatening to others" (*Bethel School District No. 403 v. Fraser*, 1986).

Next-gen negligence hasn't changed regarding these duties or legal precedents relating to student speech. However, in legislative texts it may appear that the negligence element of "injury," which some may argue could include that which is "highly offensive or highly threatening," has expanded an administrator's duty to ensure equity in the delivery of education to include responsibility for "making students feel discomfort or guilt based on their race or gender" (*Forman*, 2021). There is a fine and shifting line between speech or curricula that one may find offensive or threatening and that another may find essential to defining their views or their identity. The added challenge for administrators is to keep public education balanced between an empirically researched curriculum focused on which is best for students and that reflecting more personal parent and community sentiment.

Two landmark cases address free expression relative to published speech.

- *Board of Education, Island Trees Union Free School District No. 26 v. Pico by Pico* established, in a 5-4 decision, some guidelines for the removal of books in classrooms and school libraries. Justice William J. Brennan says in his opinion,

  [W]e hold that local school boards may not remove books from school library shelves simply because they dislike the ideas contained in those books and seek by their removal to 'prescribe what shall be orthodox in politics, nationalism, religion, or other matters of opinion.' (*Board of Education, Island Trees Union Free School District No. 26 v. Pico by Pico*, 1982, at 872)

Agreeing that the school board in this case had some control over what appears in school libraries, Justice Brennan added regarding removal of materials,

*[T]hat discretion may not be exercised in a narrowly partisan or political manner. If a Democratic school board, motivated by party affiliation, ordered the removal of all books written by or in favor of Republicans, few would doubt that the order violated the constitutional rights of the students denied access to those books. The same conclusion would surely apply if an all-white school board, motivated by racial animus, decided to remove all books authored by blacks or advocating racial equality and integration. Our Constitution does not permit the official suppression of **ideas**. Thus,*

*whether petitioners' removal of books from their school libraries denied respondents their First Amendment rights depends upon the motivation behind petitioners' actions. If petitioners **intended** by their removal decision to deny respondents access to ideas with which petitioners disagreed, and if this intent was the decisive factor in petitioners' decision, then petitioners have exercised their discretion in violation of the Constitution.* (emphasis added) (*Board of Education, Island Trees Union Free School District No. 26 v. Pico by Pico*, 1982, at 870–871)

While this clarification helps administrators to know how case law can support the decisions regarding learning resources, *Pico*, a 5-4 decision, is more important as guidance for school boards and their counsel, especially as now regards book bans. The next case, however, has a direct impact on an administrator's duties to students.

- In *Hazelwood School District v. Kuhlmeier*, a 5-3 decision about an administrator's right to censor a student publication, Justice Byron R. White wrote, "[W]e hold that educators do not offend the First Amendment by exercising editorial control over the style and content of student speech in school-sponsored expressive activities, so long as their actions are reasonably related to legitimate pedagogical concerns" (*Hazelwood School District v. Kuhlmeier*, 1988, at 273). Especially significant to our exploration of next-gen negligence are Justice White's words distinguishing,

school-sponsored publications, theatrical productions, and other expressive activities that students, parents, and members of the public might reasonably perceive to bear the imprimatur of the school. These activities may fairly be characterized as part of the school curriculum, whether or not they occur in a traditional classroom setting so long as they are supervised by faculty members and designed to impart particular knowledge or skills to student participants and audiences. (*Hazelwood School District v. Kuhlmeier*, 1988, at 271)

Of these particular activities, Justice White notes:

Educators are entitled to exercise greater control *... to assure that participants learn whatever lessons the activity is designed to teach, that readers or listeners are not exposed to material that may be inappropriate for their level of maturity, and that the views of the individual speaker are not erroneously attributed to the school.* (emphasis added) (*Hazelwood School District v. Kuhlmeier*, 1988, at 271)

Considerations about an administrator's duty to students regarding curriculum-related expression that includes publications have been clear since *Hazelwood*—that schools have an obligation to set the standards for teaching that include their professional appraisal of appropriate material for school-sponsored activities. This decision echoes that from *Fraser*, just two years before, "The determination of what manner of speech in the classroom or in school assembly is inappropriate properly rests with the school board" (*Bethel School District No. 403 v. Fraser*, 1986, at 683). The school board is the ultimate arbiter of what is taught, and administrators take their direction from the decisions of that governing body who are, ideally, guided by those they hire with training in their professional roles.

Despite publicized pending legal challenges to book bans across the country—and state legislation imposing fines *for* banning reading material as opposed to sanctions *against*—there have been few cases disputing curriculum bans. That may mean that new legislation redefining the contours of public school curricula could become a challenge for administrators in terms of whose interests the administrators serve. Are they responsible to ensure what the profession deems the students' best academic interests, or is their duty to what appears to be a loud minority of restrictive voices? And what happens to administrators when their duty to uphold the law is in conflict with what they've always accepted as the standards for their professional integrity?

A tug-of-war seems to be emerging between Supreme Court decisions in cases such as *Pierce, Meyers*, and *Yoder* (see Chap. 4) that defined a parent's control over their child's education and cases that have supported the individual rights of students and ensured protections for their unique learning needs. The question becomes who can and will speak for the students? Will we see student action against limitations on their resources for learning? To what extent can faculty speak out?

Three major cases address faculty speech.

- The 8-1 decision in *Pickering v. Board of Education* set the standard for employee speech as a "right to speak on issues of public importance" (*Pickering v. Board of Education*, 1968, at 574).
- In a 5-4 decision in *Connick v. Myers*, Justice Byron R. White clarified that "[w]hether an employee's speech addresses a matter of public concern must be determined by the content, form, and context of a given statement" (*Connick v. Myers*, 1983, at 147–148).

- And, finally, in a 5-4 decision in *Garcetti v. Ceballos*, Justice Anthony Kennedy wrote, "[T]he First Amendment does not prohibit managerial discipline based on an employee's expressions made pursuant to official responsibilities," adding the caveat that "expression related to academic scholarship or classroom instruction implicates additional constitutional interests that are not fully accounted for by this Court's customary employee-speech jurisprudence" (*Garcetti v. Ceballos*, 2006, at III).

The take-away from these cases is that teachers in the public school setting may speak out on matters of public but not private concern. This can be a fine line, especially when considering the motivation behind the new laws enacting curricular change. According to constitutional law professor Derek Black, "Although the Supreme Court has found that students have a First Amendment right to voice their opinions at school, teachers do not.... Nor do they benefit from the wide-ranging academic freedom accorded to university professors" (Natanson, 2023). Black continues, saying, "it's difficult for plaintiffs to show that curriculum restrictions violate other laws, the U.S. Constitution or precedent" (Natanson, 2023). Why court challenges are not forthcoming may thus have to do with limited resources on the part of teachers and schools to file suit, as well as perceived limitations on teachers' free expression in their professional roles.

Challenges to free expression and an administrator's duty would not be complete without consideration of how religion enters public education, an essential part of the First Amendment. In the past, the line separating church and state was fairly well-defined through a series of Supreme Court and lower court cases establishing limitations for school involvement in, for example, holiday celebrations, school prayer, and interaction with religious organizations.

Most recently, the Supreme Court's 5-3 decision in *Kennedy v. Bremerton* declared, "Respect for religious expressions is indispensable to life in a free and diverse Republic—whether those expressions take place in a sanctuary or on a field, and whether they manifest through the spoken word or a bowed head" (*Kennedy v. Bremerton*, 2022, at Section V). Justice Neil Gorsuch in his opinion and Justice Sonia Sotomayor in her dissent differ greatly in their choice and interpretation of the events leading to this case of a coach praying on the football field immediately following a game.

Deciding in favor of the coach, the Court's ruling speaks to the District's attempts to differentiate between free exercise and free speech in the First Amendment. Justice Gorsuch's opinion speaks to the challenge this decision sets before administrators:

> *In truth, there is no conflict between the constitutional commands before us. There is only the 'mere shadow' of a conflict… And in no world may a government entity's concerns about phantom constitutional violations justify actual violations of an individual's First Amendment rights.* (*Kennedy v. Bremerton*, 2022, at Section IV-B)

This implies very careful consideration on the part of administrators going forward about when that line between free speech and free expression may have been crossed in the school setting. Justice Gorsuch establishes that this line is decided based on "historical practices and understanding" (*Kennedy v. Bremerton*, 2022, at Section IV-A), which leaves administrators pondering duty and the potential for injury at the mercy of the interpretation of their district's solicitor.

A conflict of opinion evident in the First Amendment challenges facing school administrators seems to be taking us back to the meaning of public education and the responsibilities of those involved in schooling. Is an educator's role "to act as agents of social justice who encourage children to make the world a more equal place," or should educators "remain focused on basic academics … leav[ing] societal and cultural issues to parents" (Natanson et al., 2022).

In terms of next-gen negligence and the First Amendment, administrators are currently caught in the crosshairs.

References

Alvarez, B. (2023, May 25). We will not erase history. *neaToday*. https://www.nea.org/nea-today/all-news-articles/we-will-not-erase-history

Bethel School District No. 403 v. Fraser, 478 U.S. 675 (1986).

Board of Education, Island Trees Union Free School District No. 26 v. Pico by Pico, 457 U.S. 853 (1982).

Connick v. Myers, 461 U.S. 138 (1983).

Forman, C. (2021, May 7). Stitt signs controversial bill limiting race, gender curriculum in schools. *The Oklahoman*. https://www.oklahoman.com/story/news/2021/05/07/oklahoma-gov-stitt-signs-bill-censoring-race-gender-school-curriculum/4989720001/

Garcetti v. Ceballos, 546 U.S. 410 (2006).
Hazelwood School District v. Kuhlmeier, 484 U.S. 260 (1988).
Kennedy v. Bremerton, 597 U.S. ___ (2022).
Mahanoy Area School District v. B.L., 594 U.S. ___ (2021).
Morse v. Frederick, 551 U.S. 393 (2007).
Natanson, H. (2023, March 17). Few legal challenges to laws limiting lessons on race, gender. *The Washington Post.* https://www.washingtonpost.com/education/2023/03/17/legal-challenges-gender-critical-race-theory/
Natanson, H., Morse, C.E., Narayanswamy, A., & Brause, C. (2022, October 18). An explosion of culture war laws is changing schools. Here's how. *The Washington Post.* https://www.washingtonpost.com/education/2022/10/18/education-laws-culture-war/
Pickering v. Board of Education, 391 U.S. 563 (1968).
Tinker v. Des Moines Independent Community School District, 393 U.S. 503 (1969).
U.S. Const. amend. I.

CHAPTER 9

Next-Gen Negligence and Equity

Abstract Chapter 9 examines the interplay between next-gen negligence and the concept of equity in a public school setting. First, the authors distinguish equity and equality, concepts that are often confused but that have important differences, especially when contemplating the duties owed by public school employees to various stakeholders such as other employees, students, and parents. Through an examination of landmark cases, statutes, and current events, the authors engage readers in a discussion about these concepts and provide hypotheticals to help further the conversation.

Keywords Equity • Equality • Affirmative action • Title IX • Deliberate indifference • Race • Equal protection • Civil rights • Discrimination • Civics

In order to discuss equity, it's important to first understand what it is. Equity is *not* equality, though it is easy to confuse the terms. Equality is defined as "the state or quality of being equal" (Dictionary, Equality, n.d.-b), and equity is defined as "the quality of being fair or impartial" (Dictionary, Equity, n.d.-c). While similar, there is an important difference in these definitions—a difference that becomes especially important as we contemplate equity in an education setting. Equality centers around the idea of sameness, while equity centers around the idea of fairness.

A familiar visual depicts three children of different heights looking over a fence at a baseball game (see https://interactioninstitute.org/illustrating-equality-vs-equity/). The first picture depicting equality shows each perched on the same-size box enabling two of them to see the game and the third needing to look unsuccessfully through the fence boards. The second picture depicting equity shows the boxes distributed relative to each child's height enabling all to see over the fence and enjoy the game.

Although all three people in the "equality" illustration are treated equally, as they each have an apple box to boost their line of sight, they are not treated fairly, as only two of the people in the first picture can see over the fence. However, in the "equity" illustration, each child is treated fairly, with only the two needing assistance to see using an apple box, and each person using the size apple box appropriate to their need.

Equity plays an important role in public education. Demographics undoubtedly vary from state to state and district to district, and they vary within each district and school as well. Accordingly, administrators, teachers, board members, parents, and students alike must always consider equity in the judgments and decisions they make.

Affirmative action is perhaps the best-recognized example of the law's attempting to guarantee equity in education. Affirmative action is defined as "the encouragement of increased representation of women and minority-group members, especially in employment" (Dictionary, Affirmative Action, n.d.-a). Its foundation comes from the Civil Rights Act of 1964 which "prohibits discrimination on the basis of race, color, religion, sex or national origin" (U.S. Department of Labor, n.d.). The landmark case *Regents of University of California v. Bakke* in 1978 upheld affirmative action by permitting colleges to consider race as one factor (out of many) for admission, but disallowed setting specific racial quotas for incoming classes.

Commonly referred to as "Title IX," 20 U.S.C. §1681 *et. seq.* is another well-known statutory codification of equity in education. Any public school that receives federal funds must comply with Title IX which, simply put, seeks to "remove[the] barriers that once prevented people, on the basis of sex, from participating in educational opportunities and careers of their choice" (U.S. Department of Justice, n.d.). Public schools are required to both have and distribute policies that aim to prevent sexual harassment and discrimination, provide avenues for students to make complaints related to sex discrimination, and employ a Title IX coordinator in order to be in compliance with the statute (U.S. Department of Justice, n.d.). As of this writing, Title IX is in the process of being reviewed and revised under the Biden administration.

In 1977, three female Yale students became the first to sue for sexual harassment under Title IX in *Alexander v. Yale University* (1980) (Title IX Timeline, n.d.). Although their case would ultimately fail at the appeal level, this marked a change in our judicial history as far as educational equity is concerned.

Title IX cases are still prevalent today. In October 2023, a family from Leesburg, Virginia, sued the Loudon County School Board alleging their 15-year-old daughter was the subject of multiple Title IX violations, including the school's failure to keep her safe and to conduct a timely Title IX investigation, covering up her sexual assault which had occurred in a school bathroom. The Loudon County lawsuit is interesting in that it also potentially implicates issues of transgender rights, as the complaint alleges that the female student "was sexually assaulted in a women's restroom by a 'skirt wearing male,'" who, according to an independent investigation, was a male-identifying person who "wore a skirt to gain access to girl's bathrooms" (Gustin, 2023). Despite having knowledge that this particular assailant had targeted not only the victim but also other students at other schools in the district, the then-superintendent, when directly asked if such assaults "happen in restrooms and locker rooms regularly," claimed there were no "records of assaults occurring in our restrooms" (Gustin, 2023).

Expert reports presented to the grand jury revealed that not only was the then-superintendent aware of the multiple assaults, but that "the second assault could have been prevented if the division had handled the situation better" (Gustin, 2023). Examples such as this, where an administrator is allegedly aware that a student is the object of sexual harassment but chooses to do nothing or fails to act, is known as "deliberate indifference."

The concept of deliberate indifference is a direct connection we can make to an administrator's potential liability for negligence. According to the major provisions outlined in the U.S. Department of Education's Title IX Final Rule, "A school must respond **promptly** to Title IX sexual harassment in a manner that is not deliberately indifferent, which means in a way that is not clearly unreasonable in light of the known circumstances" (U.S. Department of Education, n.d., at 5).

Affirmative action also continues to be a hot topic, though most recently these cases center around issues in higher education. *Students for Fair Admissions (SFFA) v. Harvard College*, recently decided by the United States Supreme Court, was not directly about a preK-12 public school system, but a brief discussion is still warranted here. In this case, Harvard was accused of discriminating against Asian American applicants during the admission process. Harvard readily admitted that it used race as one of the factors considered in its admission process, but argued that this was acceptable because it followed the test for race-based admission as laid out in an earlier case, *Grutter v Bollinger* (*Students for Fair Admissions v. President and Fellows of Harvard College*, 2023).

Grutter held that:

> universities cannot establish quotas for members of certain racial groups or put members of those groups on separate admission tracks ... or insulate applications who belong to certain racial or ethnic groups from the competition for admission. Universities can, however, consider race or ethnicity more flexibly as a 'plus' factor in the context of individualized consideration of each and every applicant. (*Grutter v. Bollinger*, 2003)

Grutter, it seems, upheld and permitted what we can generally think of as classic affirmative action, applied in the name of equity. Think back to the description of children struggling to see the ball game at the start of this chapter. The *Grutter* opinion seems to consider race and ethnicity like the apple box upon which an applicant stands in order to get a more even footing in the application process as compared with other students. It upheld an earlier decision in the 1978 case of *Regents of the University of California v. Bakke*, which "permitted race-based considerations in order to contribute to the diversity of the student body but not to address the continued impacts of societal discrimination" (National Education Policy Center Newsletter, 2023).

The Court in *SFFA v. Harvard* reached a different conclusion, with Chief Justice Roberts writing for a 6-3 majority concluding that Harvard's race-based admissions system did not show that it avoided racial stereotypes and had a "logical endpoint for when race-based admissions would cease" (*Students for Fair Admissions v. President and Fellows of Harvard College*, 2023). Instead of allowing consideration of race as a factor in college admissions, *SFFA v. Harvard* determined that university admissions may consider an applicant's race, but only through "broader stories of [the applicant's] accomplishments, overcoming obstacles, leadership, and the like." "The focus," Chief Justice Roberts continued, "must be on demonstrated leadership or courage or other traits, experiences and the lessons learned that might help the applicants contribute to the university" (National Education Policy Center Newsletter, 2023).

You may be wondering what race-based admission concerns have to do with K-12 public schools. While admission to a specific public school, itself, may not hinge on an application, certain programs generally within the K-12 school universe may indeed have relevance to the application processes. Consider, for example, gifted and talented programs, scholarship applications, or even audition-based school activities such as fine arts extracurriculars and sports teams. School counselors and school-offered college prep courses are also impacted by the ruling in *SFFA v. Harvard* as they assist students with their application essays—essays which, in the words of the Chief Justice, may include a "discussion of how race affected his or her life, be it through discrimination, inspiration, or otherwise" (ACLU, 2023). Administrators need to ensure that students are properly advised and that course offerings support students to offer them every advantage in applying for higher education opportunities.

Equity plays an important role in cases where it may not seem readily apparent that there are issues of race, socio-economic status, or other similar issues at play. In the matter of *Gary B. v. Whitmer* introduced in Chap. 4, students in Detroit's "worst performing schools," made claims that the "conditions at the school were so poor that children were unable to attain an education and achieve literacy" (Network for Public Health Law, 2023). The conditions alleged, while not totally under the control of the administration, could implicate administrators in potential issues of negligence regarding staffing, maintenance of safe facilities, and supplying proper resources needed for learning.

Among their concerns, the plaintiffs alleged civil rights violations based on the Due Process and Equal Protection Clauses of the 14th Amendment, specifically arguing that "Defendants discriminated against Plaintiffs by failing to provide the same access to literacy they give to other Michigan students" (*Gary B. v. Whitmer*, 2020, p. 20).

While there remains no fundamental right to an education in the United States, an argument can be made that "the equal protection clause of the 14th Amendment requires that when a state establishes a public school system …, no child living in that state may be denied equal access to schooling" (Teach for Democracy n.d.). The American Civil Liberties Union (ACLU) goes so far as to state that "the Constitution requires that all kids be given equal educational opportunity no matter what their race, ethnic background, religion, or sex [is], or whether they are rich or poor, citizen or non-citizen" (ACLU, 2003).

In 1994, five low-wealth school districts in North Carolina alleged that "they have a right to adequate educational opportunities which [were] being denied [to] them ... under the current school funding system" and "that the North Carolina Constitution not only creates a fundamental right to an education, but it also guarantees that every child, no matter where he or she resides, is entitled to equal educational opportunities" (Leandro v State, 1997, at 252). The plaintiffs alleged:

> *children in their poor school districts [were] not receiving a sufficient education to meet the minimal standard for a constitutionally adequate education ... because there is a great disparity between the educational opportunities available to children in those districts and those offered in more wealthy districts* [in North Carolina]. (*Leandro v State*, 1997, at 342)

The plaintiffs claimed school facilities were inadequate with "insufficient space, poor lighting, leaking roofs, erratic heating and air conditioning, peeling paint, cracked plaster, and rusting exposed pipes" (*Leandro v State*, 1997, at 252). They further alleged:

> *media centers* [had] *sparse and outdated book collections and lack*[ed] *the technology present in the wealthier school districts* [and that] *they* [were] *unable to compete for high quality teachers because local salary supplements in their poor districts [were] well below those provided in wealthy districts,* [and that the] *inability to hire teachers cause*[d] *the number of students per teacher to be higher in their poor districts than in wealthy districts.* (*Leandro v State*, 1997, at 252)

The *Leandro* Court found that "the right to a free public education is explicitly guaranteed by the North Carolina Constitution," but questioned whether "the state is required to provide children with an education that meets some minimum standard of quality" (*Leandro v State*, 1997, at 254).

The *Leandro* court held that, yes, there is an educational right to a "sound basic education," in North Carolina. Almost as a guide for administrators in delivering this education, the court was specific in defining a "sound basic education" as:

> *one that will provide the student with at least: (1) sufficient ability to read, write, and speak the English language and a sufficient knowledge of funda-*

mental mathematics and physical science to enable the student to function in a complex and rapidly changing society; (2) sufficient fundamental knowledge of geography, history, and basic economic and political systems to enable the student to make informed choices with regard to issue that affect the student personally or affect the student's community, state, and nation; (3) sufficient academic and vocational skills to enable the student to successfully engage in post-secondary education or vocational training; and (4) sufficient academic and vocational skills to enable the student to compete on an equal basis with others in further formal education or gainful employment in contemporary society. (Leandro v State, 1997, at 255)

Fast-forward to Jersey City, New Jersey, in 2023, where the self-called "Revolutionizers of Jersey City High Schools," a group of student activists, have taken it upon themselves to complain to the School Board about broken air conditioning systems, chipping and peeling wall paint, cockroaches and rats, leaking pipes, bathrooms without functioning locks, toilet paper, soap, or paper towels, overflowing toilets and other unsanitary conditions, leaking and moldy ceilings that drip onto the students while in class, and a complete lack of arts classes and a failing sports program (Kilkenny, R., 2023a, October 21 and 2023b, November 17).

While affirmative action and Title IX violations are considered civil rights issues, elements of negligence are also at play here. Indeed, most complaints filed in our court system include more than one count—so it is entirely possible that a complaint filed against a school district for affirmative action and Title IX violations could sound both in civil rights and in negligence. Cases can be filed based upon the physical conditions in a school or district and connections between those conditions and a child's learning opportunities and success in schooling.

How can an administrator (or teacher or school board member for that matter) be negligent on issues that also implicate affirmative action or Title IX? The issue often starts in the area where an administrator (or teacher or school board member) has some element of control.

Let's consider the following example. Imagine a situation where an administrator is planning a high school curriculum in Tampa, Florida, which has a demographic breakdown as follows: 58.8% White, 22.4% Black or African American, 26.2% Hispanic or Latino, and 4.6% Asian (U.S. Census Bureau, 2022). Florida's Department of Education publishes a curriculum guide for teaching topics regarding race to high school students which includes an assessment of Jim Crow Laws, Black Codes, sharecropping, the Civil Rights Movement, and the Black Power Movement in Social Studies classes taught at the 9–12 grade levels (Florida Department of Education, n.d.). The governor plans to sign into law the Stop W.O.K.E. Act, which "codifies the Florida Department of Education's prohibition on teaching critical race theory in K-12 schools" and "prohibits school districts, colleges and universities from hiring woke CRT consultants" (Flgov.com, n.d.). There is a period for public comment on the proposed Stop W.O.K.E. Act (the "Act") of 45 days, and our Tampa-based administrator, knowing the demographic of the city where they work, fails to make any public comment about the Act, which will result in banning education on topics that affect at least nearly half of their students (48.6%). Is the administrator negligent for failing to make any public comment? What if the Act is signed into law but the administrator decides to include Critical Race Theory in their curriculum, anyway? What do you think would happen in such a scenario where the administration openly defies a codified law which is discriminatory on its face? How do you think this would play out in a state that does not have a codified Stop W.O.K.E. Act?

At this point, it becomes imperative to return to *A.C. v. Raimondo*, first mentioned in Chap. 4. This is a case in which Rhode Island public school students filed a class action lawsuit against the state, alleging their constitutional rights were violated because the state did not provide them and "other similarly situated students" with an "adequate civics education … to prepare them to function productively as civic participants capable of voting, serving on a jury, understanding economic, social, and political systems sufficiently to make informed choices, and to participate effectively in civic activities" (*A.C. v. Raimondo*, 2020, at 174). Plaintiffs based their claims on the

> *downgraded … teaching of social studies and civics, focusing in recent decades on basic reading and math instruction* [and] *limited opportunities for student involvement in co-curricular and extracurricular activities, the elimination of library media specialists, no opportunities for field trips to the state legislature, city council, or courts, no or very limited options for student participation in student governance or school affairs and no or very limited school newspapers, school sponsored speech and debate or moot court activities.* (*A.C. v Raimondo*, 2020, at 174)

Although the Court acknowledged that the *A.C.* plaintiffs "seem to recognize … that American democracy is in peril" and that "we would do well to pay attention to their plea," for an adequate civics education, the case was dismissed, as the Court had no choice but to find that there is no constitutional guarantee to a civics education (*A.C. v Raimondo*, 2020, at 192–193).

The First Circuit's anguish in having to reach such a conclusion is felt strongly throughout the opinion, and we encourage you to read the full opinion on your own time. However, a few points bear mentioning here. Specifically, the court recognized the importance of a strong civics education in maintaining a working democracy numerous times in the opinion's conclusion. The court ended its opinion by commending the plaintiffs for bringing this case as it "highlights a deep flaw in our national education priorities and policies" (*A.C. v Raimondo*, 2020, at 197). And, while the court could not rule in the plaintiffs' favor, it explicitly called on "others who have the power to address this need," to "respond appropriately," seemingly begging administrators to take the action it could not by ensuring that students receive adequate civics education and opportunities (*A.C. v Raimondo*, 2020, at 197).

We can think of negligence as the precursor to a civil rights claim. Presumably, if administrators (or teachers or school boards) fail to take action to prevent civil rights or Title IX violations, it's very possible that negligence claims can result in their school districts. Put differently, before a claim can reach the level of a civil rights or Title IX violation, there must have been some act of negligence earlier in the timeline. Thinking of these claims in such a light, do you think that the *A.C.* Court explicitly created a duty of care for (at least Rhode Island) administrators to include a basic level of education in their curricula? Did the *A.C.* Court punt us right back into the realm of negligence in such cases?

Next, consider this scenario, which draws inspiration from a real-life event: an elementary-age girl decides she wants to play sports, but not just any sport. She wants to be the kicker for the local Pee Wee football team. She is permitted to join and quickly rises to stardom, becoming the best kicker in the town. Fast-forward to high school, and our star kicker decides to try out for the boy's football team, as her school does not have a team for girls. There is no doubt that if she is permitted to try out, she would make the team with ease. However, before try-outs are held, some students get wind of her intentions and start bullying her in school, calling her derogatory names and threatening to harm her if she makes the team and "takes the spot" from a boy. Although the bullying behavior is well known among the faculty and administrators, who cannot help but overhear the chatter among the students, no one takes any action to stop them.

The female student never makes any formal reports about the bullying she endures leading up to tryouts. She tries out and makes the team and the bullies trip her in a stairwell. She falls down the stairs and sustains a season-ending ankle break.

Where is the negligence here? How would this have been different if she was not permitted to try out at all? Could the administration have avoided negligence and Title IX issues under this fact pattern? How? What control does the administration have to avoid this situation from happening?

Think back to the *Loudon* case earlier in this chapter. Do you see any potential for negligence-based claims in such a situation? The school was on notice about this particular assailant's prior history—does the failure to take action to stop future assaults result in negligence? Almost certainly. But, how would an administrator balance issues of discrimination with issues of safety? Don't forget, here we have a student seemingly trying to use a cloak of transgender rights to gain access to his victim(s). Situations like this propel us straight into the "next-gen negligence" universe. Administrators will be tasked with balancing rights of students who legitimately identify as transgender and should be afforded all the protections they are due with those students (and, potentially, parents and other community members) who seek to exploit these very sensitive issues. This remains a very open-ended and theoretical issue, as no court has yet had the opportunity to rule on what should be done in these situations.

Think now about the Jersey City Revolutionizers. While these students could almost certainly make viable claims identical to those alleged in *Leandro* and its progeny, how would the conditions seen in both *Leandro* and the Jersey City Revolutionizers' situation play out in a negligence lawsuit? Consider that many of their complaints sound in physical safety: peeling paint, rusty leaking pipes, and other similar issues that are ripe for a personal injury lawsuit. Leaving aside tort immunities, it is almost certain that, eventually, in a school riddled with similar defects such as those in *Leandro* and Jersey City's public schools, a student, teacher, administrator, or even visitor will sustain an injury as a result of the poor conditions that persist inside these school buildings. So, while equity implicates many next-gen negligence concerns, they go hand in hand with classic negligence and should not be foreign to school employees.

With all this in mind, especially including the courts' attempts to address issues of equity in public education up to now, we are still left with the reality that there is no clear line to determine where equity begins and where it has been compromised. So much is relative and left up to fluctuating factors.

In our next chapter we will explore how challenging it is for administrators to be held accountable for meeting the unique needs of all learners. While considerations of equity, fairness, and justice in the public education sphere have always been present, even results from the National Assessment of Educational Progress (NAEP), a federally administered assessment, have come up wanting in terms of providing a definition, a rubric, or any sort of hard guidelines for establishing equity. Addressing the impact of the pandemic on equity, Sarah Schwartz in *Education Week* comments that the NAEP has revealed "the uneven toll the pandemic took on student achievement. Students from low-income backgrounds fared worse than their peers, and students who were already behind saw widening gaps" (Schwartz, 2023).

Yet for those who hold COVID-19 even somewhat responsible for educational inequities, Andrew Ho from Harvard's Graduate School of Education provides the epitaph. "The real story of the pandemic," he says, "has been less about decline and recovery than it has been about inequality, inequality, and inequality." And as gaps between districts based on income increase, Ho adds, "[m]easuring gaps solely by using changes in the percent of students proficient could distort those comparisons" (Schwartz, 2023).

Among other things, equity is about perspective. And to protect themselves from litigation, administrators must learn to see through insect eyes—engaging many different lenses to anticipate and appreciate the various dimensions of equity in public education.

References

A.C. v. Raimondo, 494 F. Supp. 3d 170 (D.R.I. 2020).
ACLU. (2023, June 29). *ACLU comment on Supreme Court's ruling against Harvard and UNC's affirmative action policies* [Press release]. https://www.aclu.org/press-releases/aclu-comment-on-supreme-courts-ruling-against-harvard-and-uncs-affirmative-action-policies#:~:text=Importantly%2C%20in%20the%20opinion%20by,%2C%20inspiration%2C%20or%20otherwise
ACLU. (2003, July 17). *Ask Sybil Liberty about your right to equality in education.* https://www.aclu.org/documents/your-right-equality-education
Alexander v. Yale University, 631 F2d 178 (2d Cir. 1980).

Dictionary.com. (n.d.-a). Affirmative Action. In *Dictionary.com dictionary*. https://www.dictionary.com/browse/affirmative-action
Dictionary.com. (n.d.-b). Equality. In *Dictionary.com dictionary*. https://www.dictionary.com/browse/equality
Dictionary.com. (n.d.-c). Equity. In *Dictionary.com dictionary*. https://www.dictionary.com/browse/equity
Flgov.com. (n.d.). *Stop-Woke-Handout.pdf*. https://www.flgov.com/wp-content/uploads/2021/12/Stop-Woke-Handout.pdf
Florida Department of Education. (n.d.). *Benchmark Results: Social-studies-stands.pdf*. https://www.fldoe.org/core/fileparse.php/15223/urlt/social-studies-stands.pdf
Gary B. v. Whitmer, No. 2:16-cv-13292 (6th Cir. 2020).
Grutter v. Bollinger, 539 U.S. 306 (2003).
Gustin, A. (2023, October 6). *$30M Title IX lawsuit filed against Loudoun school board*. LoudounNow. https://www.loudounnow.com/news/30m-title-ix-lawsuit-filed-against-loudoun-school-board/article_1b04df9a-6471-11ee-99d9-1b046d9d50d8.html
Kilkenny, R. (2023a, October 21). Rats, roaches and mold: High school students slam conditions. *Jersey City Times*. https://jcitytimes.com/rats-roaches-and-mold-high-school-students-slam-conditions/
Kilkenny, R. (2023b, November 17). Student 'revolutionizers' decry 'shocking' school conditions. *Jersey City Times*. https://jcitytimes.com/student-revolutionizers-decry-shocking-school-conditions/
Leandro v. State, 488 S.E.2d 249 (1997).
National Education Policy Center Newsletter. (2023, October 26). *Students for Fair Admissions, Inc. v. Harvard College: Eight takeaways*. National Education Policy Center. https://nepc.colorado.edu/publication/newsletter-race-conscious-admissions-102623
Network for Public Health Law. (2023) *Constitutional rights and the public's health: Gary B. v. Whitmer*. https://www.networkforphl.org/resources/gary-b-v-whitmer/
Regents of the University of California v. Bakke, 438 U.S. 265 (1978).
Schwartz, S. (2023, November 1). What the latest student test results reveal: 5 things to know. *Education Week*. https://www.edweek.org/leadership/what-the-latest-student-test-results-reveal-5-things-to-know/2023/10
Students for Fair Admissions v. President and Fellows of Harvard College. *Oyez*. www.oyez.org/cases/2022/20-1199. Accessed 14 Dec. 2023.
Teach for Democracy. (n.d.). *BRIA 7 4 c Education and the 14th Amendment*. https://www.crf-usa.org/bill-of-rights-in-action/bria-7-4-c-education-and-the-14th-amendment#:~:text=While%20education%20may%20not%20be,denied%20equal%20access%20to%20schooling

Title IX Timeline: 50 Years of Halting Progress Against U.S. (n.d.). *Associated Press*. https://apnews.com/article/title-ix-timeline-5fc023ca41d7d8c2489d e24a23413938

U.S. Census Bureau. (2022, July 1). *QuickFacts: Tampa City, Florida*. https://www.census.gov/quickfacts/fact/table/tampacityflorida/PST045222

U.S. Department of Education. (n.d.). *Summary of major provisions of the Department of Education's Title IX final rule and comparison to the NPRM*. https://www2.ed.gov/about/offices/list/ocr/docs/titleix-comparison.pdf

U.S. Department of Justice. (n.d.). *Title IX Legal Manual*. Civil Rights Division. https://www.justice.gov/crt/title-ix#D.%C2%A0%20Designation%20of%20 Title%20IX%20Coordinator%20(%C3%AF%C2%BD%C2%A7%20__.135(a))

U.S. Department of Labor. (n.d.). *Legal Highlight: The Civil Rights Act of 1964*. https://www.dol.gov/agencies/oasam/civil-rights-center/statutes/civil-rights-act-of-1964#:~:text=The%20Civil%20Rights%20Act%20of%201964%20 prohibits%20discrimination%20on%20the,hiring%2C%20promoting%2C%20 and%20firing

CHAPTER 10

Next-Gen Negligence and Students' Unique Learning Needs

Abstract Chapter 10 shifts the focus from examining a public school student body as a whole to taking a closer look at the duties public school employees owe students with unique learning needs. Looking again at court decisions with which, by this point, readers should be readily familiar, the authors examine how and when an administrator may be exposed to liability for negligence with respect to meeting the needs of each and every student in the district. By further examining cases such as *Peter W.*, the authors engage the readers in a discussion of when such liability may attach and how administrators and other employees may be protected from liability with respect to addressing students' unique learning needs.

Keywords Special needs • IDEA • Gifted and talented • Basic education • Entitlements • Life-impacting • Section 504 • Accommodations • Homeschooling

The school district and its administrators have a duty to ensure that an education consistent with a state's constitution is provided for students and that the effectiveness of the education is monitored, including ensuring that state and federal legal obligations under case law and entitlements are met. For administrators, this creates a huge responsibility bookended by potential liability when considering the challenges of how schools both address and meet the learning needs of all.

Once again, the 1976 case of *Peter W. v. San Francisco Unified School District* is an interesting one as it applies to the provision of education in a public school system and those responsible for it. In this case the California Court of Appeals addressed the question "whether a person who claims to have been inadequately educated, while a student in a public school system, may state a cause of action in tort against the public authorities who operate and administer the system. We hold that he may not" (*Peter W. v. San Francisco Unified School District*, 1976).

At the time, this case set a standard in the state of California, appearing to safeguard administrators from liability for negligence regarding the provision of education. It also made clear the relationship between negligence and public policy, both clarifying factors that contribute to an understanding of tort liability. Perhaps most notable as regards an administrator's potential burden is the case's clarification of exactly how difficult it would be to prove negligence in the setting of public education given the uniqueness of each child's needs.

> *Unlike the activity of the highway or the marketplace, classroom methodology affords no readily acceptable standards of care, or cause, or injury. The science of pedagogy itself is fraught with different and conflicting theories of how or what a child should be taught, and any layman might—and commonly does— have his own emphatic views on the subject.... Substantial professional authority attests that the achievement of literacy in the schools, or its failure, are influenced by a host of factors which affect the pupil subjectively, from outside the formal teaching process, and beyond the control of its ministers. They may be physical, neurological, emotional, cultural, environmental; they may be present but not perceived, recognized but not identified. (Peter W. v. San Francisco Unified School District, 1976, at 825)*

So it quickly becomes easy to see how school administrators may be exposed to liability for negligence in providing a program that meets all students' unique learning needs but may be somewhat protected by decisions similar to *Peter W.*, if they exist. Providing for all students' needs is a herculean task in the context of public school education confined by limitations on funding, resources, and availability of qualified staff, not to mention challenges from parents who, understandably, want the best for their children. The task exists, though, and it's helpful to understand the next-gen challenges in meeting students' unique learning needs.

Special education is one of the more common Achilles' heels for school administrators when thinking about the potential for negligence. This is likely the case because providing for the unique needs of individuals is (1) costly; (2) sometimes difficult to define or address within a larger, academically diverse population; and (3) incredibly difficult to achieve but required to be measured in the same way as for students not identified as having special needs.

Additionally, the unique needs of individuals who qualify for services under the Individuals with Disabilities Education Act (IDEA) are so much more clearly defined than are those of "typical" or "normal" students, words used to describe those in the population of general education students who can achieve success learning in a traditional public school classroom. For individuals qualifying under IDEA, that specificity demands/ensures compliance under the law. Students identified as "English Language Learners" benefit from the support of enacted laws under Title III of President Obama's Every Student Succeeds Act, as well as other case law and federal and state entitlements. But "typical" students include those who may be identified as "gifted and talented" (G&T) as well as those whose learning styles meet neither IDEA qualifications nor metrics used to determine G&T. All students have unique strengths and needs of their own, yet no group of "typical" students benefits from legal support.

Even if students are determined to be "gifted and talented" by virtue of their IQ or other qualifying tests or measures, gifted education is, in most states, not protected under any law or even incorporated into the states' mandated curriculum and pedagogy. States like Pennsylvania do provide qualified students identified as gifted with a Gifted Individualized Education Plan much like students identified under IDEA (Pennsylvania Department of Education, n.d.); however, this is the exception across the country rather than the rule. The National Association for Gifted Children (NAGC) notes that neither guidance nor requirements for gifted education are provided by the federal government and that it is up to each individual state and district to address the unique learning needs of G&T students. The NAGC site provides state-by-state information regarding various aspects of gifted education, including when and how students are screened for gifted and talented programs (Rinn et al., 2022).

So how are administrators potentially liable? In the 2023 *Perez v. Sturgis Public Schools* Supreme Court decision, we see it is now within the realm of possibility for parents/students, before exhausting the procedures under IDEA for educational services deemed not received, to file suit under the Americans with Disabilities Act or other nondiscrimination laws if the relief sought is not available under IDEA. In this case the Plaintiff, Luna Perez, sought compensatory damages not available to him under IDEA for his district's failure to provide adequate and properly trained sign-language interpreters for him resulting in his ultimately being denied a diploma. While this was understandably a unanimous decision in support of the student, it potentially enhanced administrators' duties by broadening their perspective in considering whether and how students' needs are being met. And while school administrators do not necessarily sit as part of Child Study Teams tasked with creating students' programs, administrators must assume responsibility for their oversight.

Fast-forwarding to the case of *Gary B. v. Whitmer* mentioned several times thus far, we find the issue addressed of whether students have a "fundamental right to a basic minimum education, an issue the Supreme Court has repeatedly discussed but never decided" (*Gary B.*, 2020, p. 2). While the Sixth Circuit in this case did, in fact, agree that a basic minimum education should be a fundamental right, as this case was then settled by Governor Whitmer, it never went as far as the U.S. Supreme Court. This aside, whether or not education is deemed a "fundamental right" under the U.S. Constitution neither heightens nor lessens an administrator's liability for negligence. It simply reinforces a responsibility that could be viewed as a duty.

It could be argued that *Gary B.* addresses the failure to educate as a *state* responsibility in accordance with previous rulings from the Michigan Supreme Court and, thus, does not have a direct bearing on an administrator's potential liability for failing to deliver. However, Plaintiffs do mention that the Detroit Public Schools were led by administrators "with no backgrounds in education" (*Gary B.*, 2020, p. 4) as well as "teachers who lack appropriate state-mandated credentials and qualifications" (*Gary B.*, 2020, p. 7) and cite lack of professional development and resources needed to provide literacy education. While administrators are responsible for hiring quality staff, deficiencies claimed in this case significantly correlate with a lack of funding and issues that far transcend an administrator's liability for negligence. The case, having been settled, also has no precedential clout.

However, it is not difficult to imagine a world where an administrator could be held liable for failing to meet obligations in providing staffing, curriculum, and resources to comply with state constitutional guarantees for children. This would include, especially, guarantees of basic education afforded those for whom traditional public education, public education for typical children, does not suffice. Taking this argument one step further, a question arises: could failure to produce literate students actually create liability for increasing the population of children with special needs? Does this relate to a public policy that would define a duty owed? It may.

Next-gen negligence invites us into a world where nothing from the past is assured except that a law is a law until it isn't. Based upon recent U.S. Supreme Court decisions, it is clear that we can no longer take precedent or settled law from previous cases for granted.

Yet there are celebrations of entitlements that secure learning opportunities for those challenged by an ever-expanding catalog of life-impacting conditions. This includes, most recently, the effects of COVID-19, its long-term impact on health and the trauma caused by tremendous loss—both of which can affect a child's ability to learn and a school's ability to meet unanticipated and unique educational needs.

One entitlement that reached its 50-year mark in 2023 is what educators know well as Section 504 of the Rehabilitation Act of 1973. With a defined set of beneficiaries and supports that resonate in the Americans with Disabilities Amendments Act of 2008, Section 504 enables schools to go beyond IDEA in meeting learner needs as IDEA is limited to assisting students only with learning challenges in the K-12 public school setting. Section 504 affords accommodations to individuals plagued by life-impacting health conditions extending well beyond the school day and years of public education. Section 504 is what can take the place of an Individualized Education Plan (IEP) when a student moves on to college, provided the student's life-impacting condition qualifies under its terms and the student makes the institution aware of their needs.

School administrators are often outspoken when it comes to students and 504s, as the accommodation plans are known. In many schools these plans, which receive no funding to implement, can be viewed as "consolation prizes" for those who do not qualify for accommodations under IDEA and for previously identified special education students once they have successfully met their IEP goals and require only monitoring to achieve success in school. Because Section 504 carries with it minimal procedural requirements, unlike IDEA which demands timeline precision, responsibility for oversight of a student's Section 504 plan can easily get lost in the shuffle of administrative paperwork for a school leader serving as the building 504 Coordinator. Can failure to adhere to this process ultimately result in liability for negligence in ensuring a constitutionally guaranteed basic education? Perhaps. Time and circumstances will tell.

Especially in some parts of the country, there is an increasing interest from parents in homeschooling and what Harvard terms "Emerging School Models" (Harvard Kennedy School, 2023). How these alternatives to traditional public schooling affect special education and an administrator's responsibility to ensure that students identified with special needs receive a free appropriate public education (known as "FAPE" under IDEA) is unclear.

A recent *Washington Post* article noted, "Homeschooling has become—by a wide margin—America's fastest-growing form of education," and that:

> *a dramatic rise in home schooling at the onset of the pandemic has largely sustained itself through the 2022-23 academic year, defying predictions that most families would return to schools that have dispensed with mask mandates and other covid-19 restrictions.* (Jamison et al., 2023)

Homeschooled children may participate on their town's school district sports teams and in other activities. However, they are often not bound by the same academic assessments, such as state standardized tests, as children who attend public schools. The Coalition for Responsible Home Education (CRHE) shares data showing that while 24 states require accountability assessments for homeschooled children, only 9 states have assessment requirements including either *state* accountability testing or portfolios. Specific requirements in other states vary across the country (CRHE, Assessment & Intervention, n.d.-a, retrieved November 4, 2023).

As regards the provision of accommodations for children identified with special needs, the CRHE believes "that homeschooled students with disabilities should have access to testing and services provided by their local public schools at a level that is comparable to what is received by public school students" (CRHE, Frequently Asked Questions, n.d.-b, retrieved November 4, 2023). However, the U.S. Department of Education clarifies that, where FAPE is not at issue, children identified with disabilities placed by their parents in private school settings, which may include homeschooling depending upon the state,

> *do not have an individual entitlement to the special education and related services they would receive if they were enrolled in a public school or placed in a private school by the LEA* [Local Educational Agency] *as a means of ensuring FAPE is made available.* (U.S. Department of Education, 2022)

The homeschooling movement and alternatives for children with special needs can be understood from the perspective that parents want what is best for their children. If they do not feel their children are making progress in the public school setting, and especially if they have endeavored to work within the system but perceive continued efforts to be unproductive, they will understandably seek other options—even if, ultimately, their children return to public schooling.

The challenge for administrators when considering next-gen negligence is to be proactive in fostering dialogue between parents and the school such that the unique learning needs of children are addressed within the parameters of the law. Failing to do so may result in a continuing and even greater exodus of children from public schools—which will mean a loss or diversion of already stressed revenue sources and children whose needs may remain inadequately served, both in the public school setting and beyond the schoolhouse gates.

References

Coalition for Responsible Home Education. (n.d.-a). *Assessment & intervention.* https://responsiblehomeschooling.org/research/current-policy/assessment-intervention/

Coalition for Responsible Home Education. (n.d.-b). *Frequently asked questions.* https://responsiblehomeschooling.org/about/faq/

Gary B. v. Whitmer, 20a0124p.06 (6th Cir., 2020).

Harvard Kennedy School. (2023, September 28–29). *Emerging school models: Moving from alternative to mainstream* [Conference/Webinar]. https://www.hks.harvard.edu/centers/taubman/programs-research/pepg/events/emerging-school-models

Jamison, P., Meckler, L., Gordy, P., Morse, C.E., & Alcantara, C. (2023, October 31). Home schooling's rise from fringe to fastest-growing form of education. *The Washington Post.* https://www.washingtonpost.com/education/interactive/2023/homeschooling-growth-data-by-district/

Pennsylvania Department of Education. (n.d.). *Gifted Education Frequently Asked Questions.* https://www.education.pa.gov/K-12/Gifted%20Education/Pages/GiftedEducationFAQs.aspx

Perez v. Sturgis Public Schools, 598 U.S. 142 (2023).

Peter W. v. San Francisco Unified Sch. Dist., 60 Cal. App. 3d 815 (1976).

Rinn, A. N., Mun, R. U., & Hodges, J. (2022). *2020–2021 State of the states in gifted education.* National Association for Gifted Children and the Council of State Directors of Programs for the Gifted. https://cdn.ymaws.com/nagc.org/resource/resmgr/2020-21_state_of_the_states_.pdf

U.S. Department of Education. (2022). *Questions and answers on serving children with disabilities placed by their parents in private schools.* https://sites.ed.gov/idea/idea-files/questions-and-answers-on-serving-children-with-disabilities-placed-by-their-parents-in-private-schools/#_Toc96077948

CHAPTER 11

Next-Gen Negligence and Mental Health

Abstract Through an examination of various scenarios related to mental health, Chap. 11 asks readers to look to various case laws to contemplate how and when a public school district may be liable for negligence, especially as regards student mental health concerns. The authors also ask readers to contemplate the relationship between mental health and bullying, an issue prevalent in public schools, today. Finally, the authors examine the difference in anti-bullying statutes across state lines and discuss how the duties owed by administrators and other public school district employees may vary from jurisdiction to jurisdiction.

Keywords Mental health • Counseling • Special relationships • Bullying • Safety • Threats • Chaplains

Mental health is no longer the taboo subject it used to be—it is starting to take a position at the forefront of conversations about schooling, especially considering school shootings and concerns about students' engagement with social media. Questions have emerged about a school's responsibility to provide mental health services implicating administrative duties that go beyond the hushed conversations of the past. But what exactly is the responsibility of a school to protect the mental health of its students? And, what happens when a school fails to do so?

© The Author(s), under exclusive license to Springer Nature Switzerland AG 2024
B. Godett, L. M. Nobile, *Exploring Administrative Decision-Making in Public Education*,
https://doi.org/10.1007/978-3-031-58782-5_11

According to the National Center for Education Statistics (NCES), as of 2016, approximately 16.5% of children under the age of 18 in the United States suffer from at least one mental health disorder, and out of this 16.5%, about half did not receive any professional treatment or counseling (National Center for Education Statistics, 2022). NCES further found that about 55% of public schools provide "diagnostic mental health assessment services to evaluate students for mental health disorders," but that only about 42% of public schools actually offer "mental health treatment services to students for mental health disorders" (National Center for Education Statistics, 2022). Of those schools that do offer mental health treatment services to their students, about 62% offer services both in and out of school; about 30% offer services at school only; and about 7% offer services outside of school only. NCES reported that providing such services to public school student bodies poses challenges in the form of inadequate funding and poor access to mental health professionals (National Center for Education Statistics, 2022).

Although not a discussion of K-12 public schools, it has been proposed that universities could be found to have a duty to students to deliver mental health services that aim to protect the "health, safety and well being of students" (Sladdin, 2018). And, while recognizing that "the extent of a university's duties in respect of mental health has not been tested in the courts and whether a duty of care arises, or has been breached, will depend on the facts of a particular case ... there is a significant risk that if an institution fails to meet its duty to its students could lead to claims in negligence" (Sladdin, 2018). It is no stretch to imagine that such a case could not also arise in the K-12 sphere, just as it could at the higher education level.

Imagine a scenario in which a student seeks counseling at school from their assigned guidance counselor and reports that they have engaged in self-harm behavior such as cutting and having suicidal thoughts over the past few weeks. After engaging in about a 15-minute-long conversation with the student, the counselor determines that there is no immediate threat and sends the student back to class. The student goes home at the end of the day and commits suicide. (This scenario is based on one posed by William S. Friedlander of Friedlander & Friedlander, 2013).

Could the counselor or school be held liable under a theory of negligence? Friedlander compares the holding in *Armijo v. Wagon Mound Public Schools* with that of *Wyke v. Polk County School Board*. In *Armijo*, a 16-year-old special education student with mental health diagnoses had documented suicidal ideations, having previously stated to a school aide,

"[M]aybe I'd be better off dead," and to a counselor, "I'm just going to shoot myself." Both the aide and counselor knew that the student had access to firearms at home (*Armijo*, 1998, at 1256). Armijo was verbally reprimanded by his principal after harassing an elementary student, but in the presence of the principal and his counselor (who had previously heard Armijo say he would shoot himself), Armijo "threatened physical harm to the teacher that reported the [harassment incident], to the teacher's son, and to the teacher's car" (*Armijo*, 1998, at 1256–1257). Accordingly, the principal called for the immediate suspension of Armijo "on an emergency basis" and instructed the counselor to drive Armijo to his home, which the counselor did (*Armijo*, 1998, at 1257). Once at home, Armijo accessed a firearm and committed suicide—his parents returned home to find Armijo dead in his bedroom "of a self-inflicted gunshot wound to the chest from a rifle" (*Armijo*, 1998, at 1257). The school aide reported to the police that prior to his death, "Armijo was constantly depressed and nervous," and that while she told him to relax and that "everything will be ok," he replied, "I don't know ... maybe I'd be better off dead" (*Armijo*, 1998, at 1257).

Although the lawsuit that was brought against the school district did not sound in negligence but was, pled under different theories, imagine a scenario in which Armijo's parents had brought a claim against the school for negligently failing to protect their son after he expressed suicidal ideations. Leaving aside considerations of doctor/patient privilege and qualified immunity, how do you think such a lawsuit would play out? What obligations does the counselor have to encourage the parents to seek other treatment for their son? What obligations does the school have to find resources beyond what they offer at school for a student such as Armijo? How would this play out in your district?

In *Wyke*, there was, indeed, a common law negligence claim brought against the school board and principal defendants. Here, Shawn Wyke committed suicide at home on October 17, 1989, after making a first attempt the day prior while at school (*Wyke*, 1997, at 563, 564). On October 16, he was found by a fellow student, Jonathan, in the school restroom trying to hang himself with a football jersey. Jonathan was able to talk to Shawn and get him to leave the restroom; and when he got home from school, Jonathan told his mother about what happened. Jonathan's mother, Brenda, immediately called the school and spoke with

Jim Bryan, the dean of students. Mr. Bryan assured Brenda he would take care of the situation. Mr. Bryan then called Shawn to his office, read him some Bible verses, and "talked about their meaning with [Shawn]." Shawn was upset at first, but allegedly "seemed to feel better after talking with [Mr.] Bryan." Mr. Bryan took no further action, "believ[ing] that he had done all he could do with Shawn that day." He did not notify anyone else of the situation allegedly because "there was too much red tape and he thought he had it under control." However, the situation was far from "under control," because Shawn again attempted suicide in the school bathroom and eventually committed suicide on October 17, 1989 (*Wyke*, 1997, at 564).

Ultimately, the trial court concluded that the "school board negligently failed to supervise Shawn" and awarded damages (*Wyke*, 1997, at 566). The 11th Circuit affirmed, and although it limited its holding to the specific facts of this case, it stated that "when a child attempts suicide at school and the school knows of the attempt, the school can be found negligent in failing to notify the child's parents or guardian" (*Wyke*, 1997, at 571). Do you agree with this holding? Why or why not?

The answer to whether schools should be held liable for negligence in this realm is far from clear, and states are split on this very issue. Compare the holding in *Wyke* with the outcome of *Paradis v. Frost*. In *Paradis*, the school district officials were aware that a student, Jacob, "suffered from anxiety, attention hyperactivity disorder, and impulsivity" and was provided accommodations via a 504 plan (*Paradis*, 2023, at 411–12). The school also had a history of students dying by way of suicide, as five former or current students had committed suicide in the two years prior to Jacob's own death. The school counselor who worked with Jacob had made notes that three of Jacob's grandparents had passed away in 2017 and that Jacob had a friend in another district who passed from suicide. The school was further aware that Jacob had stopped doing his homework and was failing all of his classes in early 2018. Jacob's girlfriend reported to Jacob's school counselor that "she had concerns about Jacob's well-being," having observed him drinking alcohol in school, that he was "drunk, upset, and crying and that something was really wrong," and that his behavior reminded her of another who had previously committed suicide (*Paradis*, 2023, at 412). The girlfriend specifically told Jacob's counselor that she was worried that Jacob could possibly hurt himself. The counselor told the girlfriend not to worry and that she would contact Jacob's parents and the dean "to ensure that they got Jacob the help that he needed." While the counselor did thereafter meet with Jacob, she did not speak to his parents about either her meeting with Jacob or the girlfriend's concerns, and six weeks later, during summer vacation, Jacob died by suicide at home (*Paradis*, 2023, at 412).

Jacob's family brought suit alleging, among other things, that "the school district is liable for Jacob's death because the school district owed Jacob a duty to take reasonable steps to prevent his suicide" (*Paradis*, 2023, at 411–412). Here, in contrast to the Court in *Wyke*, the court concluded that the school was immune from suit and therefore was not liable. However, "for the sake of completeness," the court discussed whether such a claim would have been successful. At the outset of this discussion, the *Paradis* Court stated that "generally, there is no duty to prevent another from committing suicide. Under [Massachusetts law] we do not owe others a duty to take action to rescue or protect them from conditions we have not created" (*Paradis*, 2023, at 417, internal quotations and citations omitted).

However, the *Paradis* Court recognized that the Supreme Judicial Court of Massachusetts "recognized that special relationships may arise in certain circumstances imposing affirmative duties of reasonable care including the duty to prevent suicide" (*Paradis*, 2023, at 417, internal quotations and citations omitted). The *Paradis* Court recognized that such a duty is most typically found in public places such as jails or hospitals, and while the *Paradis* plaintiffs argued that these principles "should extend to public school districts," an argument which the court felt "has some force," they declined to make a ruling on the issue because it had already determined that the school district was immune from suit based on the Tort Claims Act (*Paradis*, 2023, at 417–418). Since the *Paradis* Court did not give us the answer to the question of whether the principles would extend to public schools, what do you think is the right call, here? Should schools be held liable for failing to protect a student from suicide?

Let's consider the obligation that public schools have to protect students, not from themselves but from other students whose actions may be taking a toll on the mental health of their peers in the form of bullying. According to Findlaw.com, while there is no federal law regarding bullying, every state has a law or policy regarding bullying, save for Montana, which has a policy discussing bullying but no actual statute prohibiting bullying. While the laws do vary across state lines, most list behaviors such as "teasing, threats, intimidation, stalking, harassment, physical violence, theft, and public humiliation" that rise to the level of bullying (Findlaw, n.d.). Some states, such as Arizona, specifically direct the governing body of *every* school to

> *prescribe and enforce policies and procedures to prohibit pupils from harassing, intimidating and bullying other pupils on school grounds, on school property, on school buses, at school bus stops, at school-sponsored events and activities and through the use of electronic technology or electronic communication on school computers, networks, forums and mailing lists....* (Ariz. Rev. Stat. § 15-341(37))

Other states such as California, which has enacted the Safe Place to Learn Act, have adopted legislation specifically discussing schools' responsibilities with respect to bullying. In California, the Safe Place to Learn Act mandates the

> *adopt[ion of] a policy that prohibits discrimination, harassment, intimidation, and bullying based on the actual or perceived characteristics [...] including immigration status [...], disability, gender, gender identity, gender expression, nationality, race or ethnicity, religion, sexual orientation, or association with a person or group with one or more of these actual or perceived characteristics.* (Cal. Educ. Code, § 234.1)

It would be far too laborious to delve into the full text of every other of the 48 states' anti-bullying statutes, but there can be no doubt this is an issue taken quite seriously all across the country. However, the existence of an anti-bullying statute does not mean there is no bullying occurring in schools from coast to coast. In fact, in what may be the "largest school bullying settlement in U.S. history," a school in California just recently at the time of drafting (September 13, 2023) settled a bullying case that resulted in the death of a bullying victim for $27 million (Taylor & Ring, 2023).

According to the attorneys, who handled the case for the plaintiff, Diego Stolz, Mr. Stolz was a "typical 13-year-old boy [...] who was the victim of constant verbal and physical bullying." He was subjected to repeated bullying at Landmark Middle School between 2018 and 2019 when he was in seventh and eighth grade, and his aunt and uncle, who raised him after his parents died, made numerous complaints to the school administrators. The bullying was so severe that at one point, Mr. Stolz was "sucker punched in the head," and although the teacher to whom he reported the incident told the assistant principal about this on the same day it occurred, the assistant principal took no follow-up action and the bullies were never suspended or otherwise disciplined for their actions, nor was the assault reported to any law enforcement agencies. The following week, Mr. Stolz was again attacked by his bullies, but when they sucker punched him this time, his head struck a concrete pillar. He sustained a traumatic brain injury, and although he was rushed to the hospital and placed on life support, he tragically died nine days later. The lawsuit that resulted alleged that "the [Landmark Middle School] District failed to enact any effective safety procedures to protect its students. The District failed to enforce its anti-bullying policies. The District negligently supervised its students. The District had a mandatory duty to properly supervise its students on campus, pursuant to the Education Code and other statutes and laws, yet failed to do so" (Taylor & Ring, 2023).

Mr. Stolz's tragic case is a clear example of bullying. But consider the following scenario (drawn from a real case based in New Jersey): A fourth-grade student, Sam, moves from a lower-middle-class neighborhood to a middle-upper-class neighborhood. At the new school, most students wear designer clothing, carry brand-name backpacks, and attend expensive after school activities. Sam, however, wears modest clothing, and an unbranded backpack, and prefers staying at home after school doing homework and reading by themselves. After a few months at the new school, Sam has not made many friends and finds themselves the target of schoolyard taunts from kids in his class aimed at teasing them for their clothes, accessories, and lack of after-school hobbies. One student repeatedly tells Sam that "quite frankly, you have no clout." Sam complains to their parents, who in turn complain to the school, alleging that Sam has become withdrawn and uninterested in their studies.

The administrators discuss the situation and ultimately conclude that the behaviors of the students taunting Sam do not rise to the level of actionable bullying and decide to take no disciplinary action but move Sam to a different class from the students who are taunting them. The taunts continue in between classes in the hallways and during communal activities such as before and after school, in the lunchroom, and during recess. Sam's parents make the decision to pull Sam from the school and enroll them in a private school, suing the public school for negligence, alleging that their failure to protect Sam from the taunts caused them to have no choice but to enroll them in private school instead.

Who wins? Did the school have an obligation to protect Sam from these taunts? Did they fail in their obligation to do so? Should they have done more? Did they do enough?

What if a student with known mental health diagnoses engages in perhaps what is the worst imaginable action and threatens to, and does, carry out a school shooting?

Let's consider a scenario that draws from another real-life example. Imagine a rural school district in western New Jersey that is made up of two middle schools and a larger high school. The eighth-grade classes from both middle schools share many friends in common and, thanks to the prevalence of social media, have developed a large eighth-grade-wide Snapchat group chat that includes students from both middle schools.

In the morning before school one day, a chat subscriber (who was already in the chat, but under an anonymous username) adds another chat subscriber to the eighth-grade-wide group, and none of the current members are able to identify the new subscribers. The newly added subscriber promptly posts a threatening message using racist language, threatening to carry out a school shooting, specifically targeting people of color and members of the LGBTQ+ community as the buses arrive at the school.

At this point in the morning, the middle school buses are already en route with some students on board, though not yet at the school. Students make their parents aware of the threat, and it is quickly reported to the administrators at both schools. School is not canceled; the buses are not instructed to turn around and bring students back home; and the students proceed to the school, albeit with additional police presence.

Luckily, in this situation, no violent acts were carried out; however, what if this threat had been legitimate, and something had happened? Do you think the school could have been held liable for negligence? Why? What should the school have done that it did not do?

Taking the scenario one step further, what if the school district acted exactly as it did, not canceling school or sending the buses home mid-route, but somehow had previous knowledge that the student who posted the threat was suffering from mental health struggles and had made previous threats that they had not carried out? What if the school was able to identify the student who posted the threat and knew they suffered from mental health struggles but had not made any threats previously?

The *Philadelphia Inquirer* recently contemplated this very issue—what does a school need to do if it learns of possible threats? According to the article, "when a school learns of a possible threat, it has to determine if the student who made it actually presents a danger." In order to do so, "schools should have good threat assessment practices in place" (Hanna, 2021). In Pennsylvania, this means that schools are required to have threat assessment teams in place "which must include people with expertise in school health; counseling; school psychology or social work; special education; school administration; and safety and security" (Hanna, 2021). Law enforcement personnel on the assessment teams are optional. According to Terri Erbacher, a school psychologist who is quoted by the *Philadelphia Inquirer* and who "served on the Pennsylvania Commission for Crime and Delinquency's committee that helped develop threat assessment guidelines," if a district is "unsure" whether a threat is innocuous (i.e., a student who, in anger, says "leave me alone, I'm going to kill you," but takes it back later, apologizing and "clarify[ying] that they weren't intending to hurt anyone and if others who are interviewed confirm that interpretation") or serious (i.e., a "threat to kill, rape, or cause very serious injury with a weapon") to "err on the side of caution."

Administrators must be vigilant when it comes to issues regarding the mental health of both students and staff. Unfortunately, funding has made adequately supporting the mental health needs of students difficult to impossible—not only in public schools, but for children and adults in society generally. Among concerns that will make school administrators even more vulnerable in meeting their duty of care for their students are an increase in teacher resignations, an already-existing teacher shortage nationwide, and states' starting to hire uncertificated staff feeling they have nowhere else to turn. Proper training is key for students to be properly served and for administrators to be able to hold staff responsible in their roles.

Additionally, recent legislation in Texas has sought to replace certified guidance counselors with chaplains. "Senate Bill 763 ... allows Texas schools to use safety funds to pay for unlicensed chaplains to work in mental health roles" (Downen, 2023). The Bill specifically states:

> *A school district or open-enrollment charter school may employ or accept as a volunteer a chaplain to provide support, services, and programs for students as assigned by the board of trustees of the district or the governing body of the*

school. A chaplain employed or volunteering under this chapter is not required to be certified by the State Board for Educator Certification. (Relating to Allowing Public Schools to Employ or Accept as Volunteers Chaplains, 2023)

Not only does this bring up First Amendment concerns regarding the separation of church and state, in terms of mental health, administrators should be concerned about their increased liability for negligence based upon the training of these chaplains, who may also include volunteers. It is currently up to individual Texas school districts to decide how to proceed.

The extent of administrative liability under next-gen negligence in this area remains to be seen.

REFERENCES

Ariz. Rev. Stat. § 15-341(37).
Armijo v. Wagon Mound Public Schools, 159 F3d 1253 (10th Cir. 1998).
Cal. Educ. Code, § 234.1.
Downen, R. (2023, May 24). Unlicensed religious chaplains may counsel students in Texas' public schools after lawmakers OK proposal. *The Texas Tribune*. https://www.texastribune.org/2023/05/24/texas-legislature-chaplains-schools/
Findlaw. (n.d.) *Specific state laws against bullying*. Findlaw.com. https://www.findlaw.com/education/student-conduct-and-discipline/specific-state-laws-against-bullying.html
Hanna, M. (2021, December 22). How should schools respond to threats of violence? Experts give tips on quelling anxiety and assessing risk. *The Philadelphia Inquirer*. https://www.inquirer.com/news/school-shooting-threats-warning-signs-safety-20211222.html
Friedlander, W.S. (2013, December). *Student suicide and school liability*. Friedlander & Friedlander. https://friedlanderlaw.com/professional-negligence/
National Center for Education Statistics. (2022, May). *Prevalence of mental health services provided by public schools and limitations in schools' efforts to provide mental health services* [Data set]. https://nces.ed.gov/programs/coe/indicator/a23/school-mental-health-services?tid=4
Paradis v. Frost, 103 Mass. App. Ct. 410 (2023).
Relating to Allowing Public Schools to Employ or Accept as Volunteers Chaplains, Texas Senate Bill 763 (2023, September 1). https://legiscan.com/TX/text/SB763/id/2817871

Sladdin, J. (2018, October 17). *Duty to care for student mental health has legal implications for universities.* Pinsent Masons Out-Law Analysis. https://www.pinsentmasons.com/out-law/analysis/duty-to-care-student-mental-health-legal-implications-universities

Taylor & Ring. (2023, September 14). *Taylor and Ring secures $27M settlement in bullying case against Moreno Valley USD.* Taylor Ring. https://www.taylorring.com/blog/taylor-ring-files-claim-against-moreno-valley-unified-school-district-for-the-death-of-a-bullied-13-year-old/#:~:text=In%20California%20Schools-,Taylor%20%26%20Ring%20Secures%20%2427M%20Settlement%20in,Case%20Against%20Moreno%20Valley%20USD&text=On%20September%2013%2C%202023%2C%20Taylor,the%20death%20of%20Diego%20Stoltz

Wyke v. Polk County School Board, 129 F3d 560 (11th Cir. 1997).

CHAPTER 12

Next-Gen Negligence and Technology

Abstract Chapter 12 takes a look at how far the use of technology as a tool for learning has come (or not) since computers were first introduced in schools. Changes to the modes of learning during COVID-19 school closures brought issues of equity front and center in terms of access and resources. Even years after the pandemic, these issues could mean increased liability for school administrators, especially when the use of government funds, or shortfalls in district funding, are challenged.

Keywords Digital • Technologies • Virtual learning • Zoom • Resources • Learning needs • Inequities • Discrimination • Internet

Back in the 1970s and 1980s when schools were first introduced to technology (think Apple II, Radio Shack TRS-80, and word processing programs such as Scripsit), teachers and administrators found themselves, perhaps for the first time, operating in a world where their students knew more than they did, at least with respect to some forms of communication. School folks were what Mark Prensky referred to as "Digital Immigrants," as differentiated from "Digital Natives" who were students growing up toward the end of the twentieth century in a world just awakening to digital technology. Prensky refers to students of this time period as "'native speakers' of the digital language of computers, video games and the Internet" (Prensky, 2001, p. 1). The digital immigrants are those Prensky notes as those "not born into the digital world but [who] have, at some later point in [their] lives, become fascinated by and adopted many or most aspects of the new technology" (Prensky, 2001, pp. 1–2).

Computer video games can be traced back to the 1960s with probably the most familiar being "Pong," emerging in 1972. Consoles such as those made by Atari hit the market in the late 1970s and early 1980s along with the rise of home computers that were affordable and of a reasonable size. Nintendo made its first appearance in 1985 (Smithsonian, n.d.). These became a most popular pastime for students and, in some cases, for adults as well!

However, even with the advent of innovative technologies, schools still operated as they had previously with a fair amount of skepticism at these newfound platforms. This was hardly surprising as schooling, like any institution or societal convention of such size, reach, and impact, is very slow to change. Citing Alfred Bork in Robert Taylor's *The Computer in the School: Tutor, Tool, Tutee* (1980), Plato, who was also not a fan of lecturing as a mode of education, reacted even to the invention of writing as a "catastrophe in human history, killing the oral tradition and killing mental training in remembering" (Godett, 1986, p. 10). Johannes Gutenberg's invention using moveable type to print books in the 1400s was an upheaval in a world where knowledge was shared through an oral tradition and writings were viewed with skepticism as forgeries (Teach Democracy, 2009).

School administrators of the later part of the twentieth century, even of the early part of the twenty-first century, had much to learn to keep pace with the manner in which, and the speed with which, their students processed information. In Prensky's words, "Our students have changed radically. Today's students are no longer the people our educational system was designed to teach" (Prensky, 2001, p. 1). There is no question that accepting this reality would have an impact on both the dimensions of an administrator's duty and the scope of what could be understood as an injury resulting from a breach of such duty.

Fast-forward to the present day—specifically 2020 when COVID-19 resulted in shuttered schoolhouses and living rooms turned into classrooms. Prensky's words remarkably still hold true: our students have changed radically, especially living through the transition from in-person to virtual learning platforms. Our teachers have been changed as well. Literally overnight, teachers were dismissed from their classrooms to

Zoom rooms, leaving them without their accustomed resources; without knowledge of how supplemental services would be offered to students who qualified for those services; and without prior training in instructional strategies that would have prepared them for a classroom where not only are they as teachers physically distanced from their students, but their students are removed from one another. And all this while keeping in mind public school's characteristic inertia and lack of resilience over time!

Teachers and administrators were hard-pressed to cope with the changes to schooling brought on by COVID-19 and the speed of the changes. Even before the shift to virtual learning could proceed, administrators found themselves struggling to provide needed consistency in technology and Internet access to all students, regardless of what technology and connectivity were available to students at home.

Would failure to do this on an equitable basis constitute liability for negligence on the part of a school administrator? Well, consider the elements of traditional negligence—duty, breach, causation, and damages. And consider what we have defined as next-gen negligence: "the application of a traditional negligence framework to new and ever-evolving injuries in fact." Regarding liability for next-gen negligence in the area of technology, an administrator's responsibility for providing education to meet the learning needs of all students may be where administrators are most vulnerable.

Under both definitions, that of traditional negligence and next-gen negligence, the administrator's duty to provide education for all students, despite the changed circumstances, would not change. Understanding that the administrator endeavored to maintain the school program and services within the district's limitations, breach might take on several dimensions, but most, if not all, could be beyond the administrator's control. The ever-evolving injuries in fact under next-gen negligence, even several years post-COVID-19, may yet to be realized.

Regarding the potential for breach, a district might not have previously acquired technology resources and funding for additional technology, especially if computers were not normally provided for each individual student. Under the Elementary and Secondary School Emergency Relief Fund (ESSER) initiated in March 2020, schools received grant monies "to address the impact that COVID-19 has had, and continues to have, on elementary and secondary schools across the Nation" (U.S. Department of Education, n.d.). Full details as to how this money was spent in each state can be found at https://covid-relief-data.ed.gov, the site for the

U.S. Department of Education's Education Stabilization Fund (see, e.g., https://www.edweek.org/policy-politics/look-up-how-much-covid-relief-aid-your-district-is-getting/2021/09). Although funding was not immediately available at the start of COVID-19, it could be assumed that administrators did their due diligence to make schooling happen with whatever resources could be creatively employed prior to the disbursement of the grants and with that aid when it became available.

So, without breach, there could be no causation leading to damages—right? Well, injury has been alleged by parents of students who they claim suffered setbacks in their learning based upon the district's inability to effectively provide, a free appropriate public education (FAPE under IDEA) in the case of students identified with special needs, and in other circumstances where there have been allegations of misappropriation of federal grant monies (see, e.g., Erica Green's (2020) *DeVos Funnels Coronavirus Relief Funds to Favored Private and Religious Schools*, mentioned in the resources for this chapter).

One case, a class action suit in New York City, was filed by parents of students with special needs for failure to provide compensatory services in accordance with IDEA (*Z.Q. et al. v. New York City Department of Education et al.*, 2022); however, in this suit defendants did not include school administrators but rather the New York City Department of Education, the New York City Board of Education, Chancellor of the New York City School District, the New York State Education Department, the New York State Board of Regents, and the Interim Commissioner of Education. What can be derived from this as well as other cases, when it comes to having control over the particulars, is that school administrators are often caught in the middle. As much as this can be protective, it can sometimes increase their vulnerability.

Liability for the provision of technology or lack thereof has been an area unanticipated and, as yet, potentially unexplored for administrators both during COVID-19 and beyond. It is important not to count this out, however. In cases we've mentioned, such as *Gary B. v. Whitmer*, (2020) students have alleged their schools/districts have not equipped them with the resources necessary to achieve a basic level of literacy—resources which, in today's world, could easily include technology. Plaintiffs in *Leandro v. State*, another case we've previously mentioned, allege that school district disparities include that their children's schools "**lack the technology** present in the wealthier school districts" (emphasis added) (**Leandro v. State**, 1997, at 252).

The impact of COVID-19 on learning even to this day is still difficult to quantify in terms of next-gen injury. Protection for school administrators who could be accused of failing to properly address students' learning needs by providing the most appropriate resources is neither anticipated nor easily proven, especially as related to technology and what the administrator can or cannot control. It is important to consider, however, that under Title VI of the Civil Rights Act of 1964 schools are required to

> *provide students with equal access to educational resources without regard to race, color, or national origin. These educational resources include, for example, access to safe school facilities,* ***instructional materials and technology****, and skilled educators. This protection remained in place through the pandemic.* (emphasis added) (Goldberg, 2021, p. 51)

In Acting Assistant Secretary for Civil Rights Goldberg's report, *Education in a Pandemic: The Disparate Impacts of COVID-19 on America's Students*, we are referred to a Dear Colleague Letter issued by the Office of Civil Rights (OCR) during the Obama administration, which we are told still applies today. That document speaks to inequities in access to education resources, particularly in districts with racially marginalized populations. Of note is that:

> *Chronic and widespread racial disparities in access to …* ***modern technology and high-quality instructional materials*** *further hinder the education of students of color today.* (emphasis added) (Lhamon, 2021, p. 2)

The Dear Colleague Letter goes on to note that:

> *Students of color must not be consigned to dilapidated, overcrowded school buildings that lack essential educational facilities …* ***and that may not be able to support the increasing infrastructure demands of rapidly expanding educational technologies*** *while providing better facilities for other students. … In addition to facilities,* ***access to instructional materials and technology for students and teachers can impact the quality of education as well as students' ability to engage with digital resources outside the classroom. Technology and other instructional tools and materials*** *support teachers in properly delivering, enhancing and personalizing the curriculum. Access to these important instructional resources varies between high-poverty schools that are heavily populated with students of color and more affluent schools serving fewer students of color.* ***While gaps by race and income in student access to technology are narrowing at a national level, disparities persist regarding***

the number and quality of computers or mobile devices in the classroom, speed of internet access, and the extent to which teachers and staff are adequately prepared to teach students using these technologies. (emphasis added) (Lhamon, 2021, pp. 4–5)

The Dear Colleague Letter shares guidelines by which intentional discrimination is measured—discrimination that could lead to accusations of negligence on the part of administrators. These guidelines can continue to serve administrators well in determining liability in this next-gen world not only as we discuss technology in this chapter, but also in other areas of potential negligence as well.

1. *Did the school district treat a student, or group of students, differently with respect to providing access to educational resources as compared to another similarly situated student, or group of students, of a different race, color, or national origin…?*
2. *Can the school district articulate a legitimate, nondiscriminatory, educational reason for the different treatment? If not, OCR could find that the district has intentionally discriminated on the basis of race. If yes, then*
3. *Is the allegedly nondiscriminatory reason a pretext for discrimination. If so, OCR would find the district has intentionally discriminated on the basis of race.* (Lhamon, 2021, pp. 6–7)

To apply these guidelines, OCR would "examine evidence regarding the quality, quantity, and availability of critical education resources…to determine whether there are disparities among schools serving similarly situated students or among similarly situated students within the same school" (Lhamon, 2021, p. 7). School districts would then be provided an opportunity to explain. OCR would also look at district policy. The Dear Colleague Letter assigns responsibility to school administrators specifically, identifying school leaders as "fostering teacher effectiveness and overall school success" (Lhamon, 2021, p. 15).

In terms of technology, the Dear Colleague Letter goes on to note the importance of technology in contributing

to improved educational outcomes and promot[ing] technological literacy and looks at comparable access to technological tools, implementation, and support, including *availability and speed of internet access* as well as teacher training, and *the extent to which students have access to necessary technology outside of school and how school districts support students who do not have internet access at home, such as through providing wireless access via a Wi-Fi hotspot at school that is available outside of school hours.* (Lhamon, 2021, pp. 18–19)

Keeping all this in mind, it is conceivable that administrators could bear responsibility and be liable for failing to provide equitable access to technology for learning, both as related to learning during COVID-19 and beyond—based upon educational outcomes. While this would have been more obvious during COVID-19 school closures, the information and procedures shared in the Dear Colleague Letter are worthy of consideration.

Also worthy of consideration, though, is that liability for negligence could be contingent upon an assigned standard for certain educational outcomes—outcomes that could be argued relate to the provision of technology. Courts have been clear that there is no guarantee of a level of achieved competence in learning beyond that guaranteed in a state's constitution, which would imply that liability for negligence in this area would be based upon specific evidence plaintiffs could provide to the contrary. From *Leandro*,

> *The principal question presented ... is whether the people's constitutional right to education has any qualitative content, that is, whether the state is required to provide children with an education that meets some minimum standard of quality. We answer that question in the affirmative and conclude that the right to education provided in the state constitution is a right to a sound basic education. An education that does not serve the purpose of preparing students to participate and compete in the society in which they live and work is devoid of substance and is constitutionally inadequate.* (*Leandro*, 1997, at 254)

The bottom line regarding next-gen negligence and technology is that administrators must be able to show they have done their due diligence regarding supplying technology and the means to access it when it comes to their duty to provide learning opportunities that meet the needs of their students, despite unusual or unimagined circumstances.

How might an administrator be vulnerable under the following scenario: A district or school decides to eliminate a program from its curriculum for any one of a number of reasons. The program may have been an elective that was not drawing enough student interest. The course may be one where it is difficult to enlist a certified teacher. The state curriculum requirements may provide little space in the school day or week.

There is technology available at no or little cost to the district that would enable students to participate in the course or program determined to be eliminated. The administrator elects not to make that technology available.

Would the administrator potentially be liable for negligence for failing to use technology if that is the only way to provide diverse educational opportunities for students? As you mull think over, think of the defenses the administrator might present such as lack of space, supervision, or available technology.

Also consider that this scenario is actually a very real one concerning the vulnerability of world language curricula throughout the country. Despite some state standards that require the study of a world language, schools are making choices to eliminate certain languages from the curriculum, and technology is available to teach world languages.

> [S]o *few students in the United States—just 20 percent—study a foreign language at the K-12 level....Only 58 percent of middle schools and 25 percent of elementary schools offer*[ed] *a foreign language in 2008, according to a 2017 report by the Commission on Language Learning, which was formed in response to a request by Congress to look deeper into foreign language learning in the United States.* (Stein-Smith, 2019)

So what do you think? Would an administrator be subject to potential liability for not making available technology that would enhance/provide learning opportunities for students?

In this particular example of world language acquisition, it may be helpful to be aware of the position statement of the American Council on the Teaching of Foreign Language (ACTFL), the *Role of Educators in Technology-Enhanced Language Learning*, which states, "Research does not support the isolated use of technology for acquiring a language" (ACTFL, 2017). Indeed, there are many things to consider when assessing the potential for administrative liability in a given situation!

The following challenges regarding technology and schooling relate to next-gen negligence. While the duty remains the same, think about whether these questions may present a change in what might be considered "injury"?

- Is the duty to provide educational opportunities for all students breached if an administrator is unable to manage a pedagogical paradigm shift such as occurred during COVID-19 school closures?
- What is the limit to the expectations for that duty?
- As regards technology, could injury be proven in any quantifiable way to show significant levels of learning loss, as some have claimed happened during COVID-19, or a loss of learning opportunities that may be available in similarly situated schools or districts?

These and other questions will be meaningful as we work toward the final chapter of our next-gen exploration addressing the responsibilities of school administrators and projections for the future of public education vis-à-vis new technologies.

REFERENCES

ACTFL. (2017, May 19). *Position statement: Role of educators in technology-enhanced language learning*. The American Council on the Teaching of Foreign Language. https://www.actfl.org/news/the-role-of-technology-in-language-learning#:~:text=Through%20the%20purposeful%20use%20of,speakers%20of%20the%20target%20language

Gary B. v. Whitmer, No. 18-1855 (6th Cir. 2020).

Godett, B. (1986). *Computer use in education: From goals to realities* (Unpublished doctoral dissertation). Lehigh University.

Goldberg, S. (2021). *Education in a pandemic: The disparate impacts of COVID-19 on America's students*. U.S. Department of Education Office for Civil Rights. https://www2.ed.gov/about/offices/list/ocr/docs/20210608-impacts-of-covid19.pdf

Green, E. (2020, May 15). DeVos Funnels Coronavirus Relief Funds to Favored Private and Religious Schools. *The New York Times*. https://www.nytimes.com/2020/05/15/us/politics/betsy-devos-coronavirus-religious-schools.html

Leandro v. State, 488 S.E.2d 249 (N.C. 1997).

Lhamon, C. (2021). *Dear colleague letter: Resource comparability*. U.S. Department of Education Office for Civil Rights. https://www2.ed.gov/about/offices/list/ocr/letters/colleague-resourcecomp-201410.pdf

Prensky, M. (2001). Digital natives, digital immigrants. *On the Horizon* 9(5). https://www.marcprensky.com/writing/Prensky%20-%20Digital%20 Natives,%20Digital%20Immigrants%20-%20Part1.pdf

Smithsonian. (n.d.). *Video game history.* https://www.si.edu/spotlight/the-father-of-the-video-game-the-ralph-baer-prototypes-and-electronic-games/video-game-history

Stein-Smith, K. (2019, February 6). *Foreign language classes becoming more scarce.* American Academy of Arts & Sciences. https://www.amacad.org/news/foreign-language-classes-becoming-more-scarce

Teach Democracy (formerly the Constitutional Rights Foundation). (2009, Winter). *Gutenberg and the printing revolution in Europe.* Teach Democracy. https://www.crf-usa.org/bill-of-rights-in-action/bria-24-3-b-gutenberg-and-the-printing-revolution-in-europe

U.S. Department of Education. (n.d.). *Elementary and secondary school emergency relief fund.* https://oese.ed.gov/offices/education-stabilization-fund/elementary-secondary-school-emergency-relief-fund/

Z.Q. et al. v. New York City Department of Education et al., Z.Q. v. N.Y.C. Dep't of Educ., No. 1:20-CV-9866-ALC, 2022 U.S. Dist. LEXIS 55956 (S.D.N.Y. Mar. 28, 2022).

CHAPTER 13

Next-Gen Negligence and Governance

Abstract Chapter 13 speaks to an administrator's potential for liability in two key areas of governance—agencies and funding. This chapter addresses the important role agencies play in protecting our citizens and agencies' increasing vulnerability based upon U.S. Supreme Court decisions threatening to cede their authority to Congress. There are many agencies that support education and validate administrative decision-making. Also in this chapter is a brief discussion of how private interest groups may be compromising the funding and future of public schools through increased support for choice and for their heightened influence in politics and school governance.

Keywords Government • Standards • Agencies • Authority • AI • Regulation • Protections • Funding • Schooling alternatives • Politicization • Curriculum • Extremist groups

There are at least three ways to view the government's relationship to public schooling and related legal matters. One is that the government can be too intrusive; another is that the government is not involved enough; and the third is that the government knows its place when it comes to education. Most people would likely subscribe to each of these three perspectives depending upon the issue, the time, and the place. Suffice it to say that federal and state governments play distinct roles in setting guidelines that, among other things, protect the rights of students and staff; set standards for school infrastructure including building code regulations, staff licensure, and curriculum; and attempt to hold schools accountable to state constitutional guidelines.

Of late, however, some state governments and the U.S. Congress are being viewed by some as interlopers in a world where their actions are potentially more harmful than beneficial. This includes government actors who have assumed an outsized role in making decisions about curriculum and learning resources, leaving educators, who normally have the training and the responsibility to make those decisions, balancing their integrity with their desire and need to maintain their employment. It is hardly an understatement to say that politically motivated changes to public education leave administrators vulnerable to liability for negligence.

THE ROLE OF AGENCIES

While this may be something educators have not noticed, especially at the building level, agencies play an outsized role in funding and infrastructure support for public schooling. One need only do a cursory scan of the *A-Z Index of U.S. Government Departments and Agencies* (n.d.) to note how agencies are engaged with many services that students and educators may take for granted. Simply looking at the agency listings A through D reveals, among others, the Administration for Children and Families, the Center for Parent Information and Resources, the Center for Disease Control and Prevention, the Centers for Medicare and Medicaid Services, and the Department of Education Office of Civil Rights.

Recent Supreme Court cases expose a chipping away of the authority of government agencies—a key support for public education. Evidence of this happening and potentially continuing is seen through the Supreme Court's defining a "major questions doctrine" which came out of the Court's 2022 case, *West Virginia v. Environmental Protection Agency* (2022). The ruling in that case severely limited the decision-making authority of the Environmental Protection Agency to regulate greenhouse gas emissions. The Court employed its new "major questions doctrine" to require administrative agencies to "point to 'clear congressional authorization' when they claim the power to make decisions of vast 'economic and political significance'" (Levin and Wheeler, 2023). This doctrine has the power and the potential to restrict efforts by agencies to offer protection to institutions such as public education that are dependent upon administrative guidance and support. Under this new doctrine, the politics of the legislature rather than the expertise of those employed by the various agencies has the greater potential to control.

One such example of impending concerns is the recent bipartisan efforts of Senators Lindsey Graham and Elizabeth Warren to create a new agency, "a Digital Consumer Protection Commission designed to ... 'prevent online harm, promote free speech and competition, guard Americans' privacy and protect national security'" (Levin and Wheeler, 2023). This effort comes in direct response to a perceived need to regulate AI, which would be easy to see as beneficial for school administrators. In a *New York Times* op-ed, the senators speak of the need for their proposed agency to address a "dark side" of digital innovation that brings with it "new avenues of proliferation for the sexual abuse and exploitation of children, human trafficking, drug trafficking and bullying and have promoted eating disorders, addictive behaviors and teen suicide" (Graham and Warren, 2023). Will this pass muster under the major questions doctrine? Only time will tell.

Agencies are an important part of our government's executive branch for many reasons, not the least of which is that they are, in part, staffed by those with expert knowledge and training in the agencies' area of concern and responsibility. Since the decision in *West Virginia v. Environmental Protection Agency*, agency actions have been overridden in housing, ending a moratorium on residential evictions in the Center for Disease Control's efforts to limit the spread of COVID; vaccinations, overturning the authority of the Occupational Safety and Health Administration to mandate vaccines for workers; and student loans, ruling against the Secretary of Education's authority to enact student loan forgiveness measures (links in Levin and Wheeler, 2023).

Whether or not the U.S. Supreme Court will continue to use the major questions doctrine to curb the authority of agencies remains to be seen. If this trend continues, however, administrators inevitably stand to lose some of the protections shielding them from liability for doing the work they need to do.

Considerations Related to Funding

Money is the glue that holds together the institution of public education as we know it. Without funding, schools are unable to support teachers and provide resources for learning. Essentially, funding is what drives innovation and the ability for the *business* of educating our youth to remain competitive with advances in science and in society, including and especially the continuation of our democracy.

The 1973 U.S. Supreme Court case *San Antonio v. Rodriguez* reaffirmed the importance of local control in education, grounded in funding, absolving the courts from responsibility for inequities among students marginalized by wealth and race. This decision, which is often still debated but yet to be overturned, reaffirmed that though the importance of education is universally recognized, that recognition goes only so far. In its 5-4 decision, Justice Lewis F. Powell Jr. declared, "Education, of course, is not among the rights afforded explicit protection under our Federal Constitution. Nor do we find any basis for saying it is implicitly so protected" (San Antonio v. Rodriguez, 1973, at 35).

However, as evidenced by cases such as *Gary B.* and *Leandro*, mentioned in our earlier chapters, it is clear that we are starting to hold states accountable for shortfalls in student learning. Parents of students are frustrated, and they are taking these frustrations out on the districts. Individual administrators are largely unscathed in terms of negligence but have been left to pick up the pieces as parents opt for schooling alternatives through homeschooling and in private and parochial schools. These options have only added to the funding issues plaguing public schools as "the money follows the child" when they leave. The exodus of students leaves behind those whose parents cannot afford to pay for a preK-12 education (as even tax credits and vouchers do not cover the bill completely), and students with special needs who would not, in most cases, be afforded the accommodations, services, and protections under federal and state statutes in private and even charter settings. But to the vulnerable, even unproven options appear as viable, desirable solutions.

Make no mistake, though. There is an impact. Perhaps the most publicized these days is the funding of public schools in Florida and the goal of current legislators for the future. Manny Diaz, Florida's Commissioner of Education as of this writing, speaks of public education as being controlled by "education elites," a "broken movement not serving the needs of our kids" (Diaz, 2023). Miami, he boasted, has 70% attending schools of choice, over 700 charters serving the state with over 300,000 kids attending (Diaz, 2023). The charters of which Commissioner Diaz speaks, however, are not the traditional public school charters. Today in Florida they include what he refers to as "out of state operators" that bring in uncertified teachers. According to Diaz, "the ultimate arbiter of the success of choice is whether the parent is happy. [We] don't judge the success of schools of choice programs the same way you gauge success of public schools" (Diaz, 2023).

What this points to and what is most concerning is the politicization of public education that has infiltrated and tainted funding schemes put in place by state constitutions with the new message that public schools will only become better when there is competition nearby. That is certainly one perspective that could apply to any situation where options exist. However, when the objective is, as Commissioner Diaz says, "We have to get these programs to the point that if we lose elections, you can't rip them away from kids" questions need to be asked about the qualifications of those building the plane (to draw from the analogy in the previous section) (Diaz, 2023).

One issue of grave importance (in addition to the creation of schooling alternatives) is how valuable resources are being spent to insert politics into the traditional public school setting. For example, a wealthy Bucks County suburb of Philadelphia, the Pennridge School District, recently adopted a new social studies curriculum brought to the district by Jordan Adams, whose company, Vermilion Education, serves only that district receiving an hourly rate of $125 with "no limit on the number of hours no specific deliverables, and no termination date" (Legum and Crosby, 2023). The curriculum adoption for which the district recently paid $7500 (Legum, 2023) derives from the 1776 Curriculum of Hillsdale College, "a private Christian institution that promotes right-wing ideologies" (Legum and Crosby, 2023). Although unqualified to write curriculum and without a background in education, Adams convinced the Pennridge Board of Education to change its approach to teaching social studies and history, despite challenges from the district's own administrators and academic experts and, indeed, national experts saying that the changes are not age-appropriate and are replete with inaccuracies that disregard context and facts. The district's adoption of this new curriculum passed with a 5-4 vote. But school boards change, and administrators should not be expected to file away their challenges—or their responsibilities to their students.

Do we appear to stray from our topic at hand—negligence on the part of school administrators? Not really. Consider these scenarios:

A non-Christian student who attends Pennridge High School takes issue with the newly implemented curriculum. Do they have the right to stand up based upon a duty owed to them because they opted for a public school versus a private school education?

Perhaps there is something particularly egregious in this new curriculum, such as an emphasis on teaching creationism rather than evolution. What happens to the student who doesn't receive what they consider to be a quality education because of curriculum such as this? Do they have a negligence claim once they reach the age of majority and realize they have not been properly or fully educated?

While these scenarios and the story from Pennridge are clearly about curriculum, they are also clearly about how money is spent to educate students and whose responsibility it is to make those decisions. By all counts, the details in reports such as this from Pennridge suggest that administrators, even in the face of some loud voices that appear to have acquired power over what is being taught in public schools, *are*, in fact, addressing their duty to provide students with an education that meets the provisions of state constitutions. Speaking up, using their voices supported by their expertise, may appear of little consequence depending upon the level of crowd noise in the background, but these actions can be significant, nonetheless.

Voters are listening. One of the actors, either behind the scenes or directly in decisions such as those being taken in Pennridge and other school districts, is Moms for Liberty (M4L), a group founded by former Florida school board members. The Southern Poverty Law Center (SPLC) which tracks extremist groups across the nation has identified them as such, calling M4L

> *a far-right organization that engages in anti-student inclusion activities and self-identifies as part of the modern parental rights movement. The group grew out of opposition to public health regulations for COVID-19, opposes LGBTQ+ and racially inclusive school curriculum, and has advocated book bans.*
> (SPLC, n.d.)

The SPLC list of ways M4L have attempted to insert themselves into school governance connects with some of the potential issues of negligence we have explored in this book. Their mission, as that of other groups like theirs, clearly puts administrators on the defensive regarding the duty owed to their students.

It is difficult to determine the impact that M4L will have on public education in the future. Brookings research notes their presence, especially in blue and purple states, and estimates their membership at "about 103,000 members across 278 chapters in 45 states" (Sinha et al., 2023). To put this in perspective, the Brookings study reports that the National Education Association (NEA) and the American Federation of Teachers (AFT), collectively, have a membership of almost five million. M4L membership, in contrast, is closer in comparison to the membership of the Massachusetts Teachers Association which boasts 117,000 members (Sinha et al., 2023). It is of note that candidates endorsed by M4L in the 2023 mid-term elections were largely unsuccessful.

On the potential of M4L to be a force against public education in the future, Brookings research notes that engaging with stakeholders locally can certainly help elect board members and pass policies consistent with the organization's beliefs and mission. However, "Moms for Liberty is such a polarizing organization, with such an extreme set of positions, that its long-term impact remains uncertain" (Sinha et al., 2023).

So what does control over the politics of school funding mean—not only for the future of public education but also for the duty of school administrators to provide an education consistent with their state constitutions and with what those most knowledgeable in the field say is best for children? It means that school administrators, to ensure they are safe from liability, must be attuned to the world around them—now, more than ever. They must be able to anticipate challenges and be prepared not only with training and knowledge, but also as models of integrity and excellence respected for their veracity and for their ability to foster trust among all school stakeholders. They must also be ready to pivot to meet unexpected challenges of the future.

REFERENCES

A-Z index of U.S. government departments and agencies. (n.d.). USAgov. https://www.usa.gov/agency-index/c#C

Diaz, Jr., M. (2023, September 29). *Opening remarks* [Speech]. Emerging School Models: Moving from Alternative to Mainstream. Harvard Kennedy School, Cambridge, MA. https://www.hks.harvard.edu/centers/taubman/programs-research/pepg/events/emerging-school-models

Graham, L. & Warren, E. (2023, July 27). When it comes to big tech, enough is enough. *The New York Times*. https://www.nytimes.com/2023/07/27/opinion/lindsey-graham-elizabeth-warren-big-tech-regulation.html?utm_source=sendgrid&utm_medium=email&utm_campaign=Newsletters

Legum, J. (2023, November 9). *UPDATE: School board voters fight back*. Popular Information. https://popular.info/p/update-school-board-voters-fight?utm_campaign=email-half-post&r=h4g2z&utm_source=substack&utm_medium=email

Legum, J. & Crosby, R. (2023, September 7). *Pennsylvania school district requires social studies classes to incorporate right-wing propaganda*. Popular Information. https://popular.info/p/pennsylvania-school-district-requires

Levin, B. & Wheeler, T. (2023, September 6). *The Supreme Court's major questions doctrine and AI regulation*. Brookings. https://www.brookings.edu/articles/the-supreme-courts-major-questions-doctrine-and-ai-regulation/

San Antonio v. Rodriguez, 411 U.S. 1 (1973).

Sinha, S., Zerbino, N., Valant, J., & Perera, R. (2023, October 10). *Moms for liberty: Where are they, and are they winning?* Brookings. https://www.brookings.edu/articles/moms-for-liberty-where-are-they-and-are-they-winning/

SPLC. (n.d.). *Moms for Liberty*. Southern Poverty Law Center. https://www.splcenter.org/fighting-hate/extremist-files/group/moms-liberty

West Virginia v. Environmental Protection Agency, 597 U.S. ___ (2022).

CHAPTER 14

Next-Gen Negligence and Unexpected Challenges

Abstract Chapter 14 looks at how next-gen negligence may arise in a public school setting due to challenges we may not readily think of as arising in a schooling environment. Social media and influencers, COVID-19, entertainment masquerading as news, imaginative play, and indeed parents and students both seeking a more involved role in education are all discussed, with the authors asking readers to think outside the box about how each of these unexpected challenges may indeed result in claims of negligence. Through a presentation of topical examples and hypothetical discussion prompts, these unexpected challenges are explored.

Keywords Social media • COVID-19 • Technology • Videotaping • Cell phones • Teacher-influencers • Holocaust education • TikTok • Curricula • In loco parentis

There has been a seismic shift in how negligence is viewed in a public school setting. This directly ties into the standards by which the American public holds administrators, faculty, and other school staff. Now, more than ever, the public has a more direct view of the classroom. This is due in no small part to the evolution and ready availability of technology, the rise of social media (particularly, the prevalence of the "(uninformed) influencer"), COVID-19, entertainment masquerading as news, parents taking a more active role in their children's education, students taking a more active role in their own education, and completely unexpected sources such as imaginative play. There are countless ways that these, and other, unintended sources can impact public education and the role that next-gen negligence plays in the public school setting. We share the below examples as some of the more prevalent. As you think about these examples of unexpected sources and next-gen negligence, what else comes to mind?

Technology and its direct relationship to curriculum and pedagogy is undoubtedly the proverbial double-edged sword. On one hand, the use of technology in the classroom helps to enhance lessons and the school experience in general in previously unthinkable ways. For example, in an art history class taught not even ten years ago, a teacher may only have had the resources to rely upon reproductions of famous art pieces in a textbook for purposes of instruction. However, now a simple Google search for "free art museum tours" brings up tours at the British Museum in London, the Guggenheim in New York, the National Gallery of Art in Washington, DC, the Musée d'Orsay in Paris, the National Museum of Modern and Contemporary Art in Seoul, Pergamon Museum in Berlin, Rijksmuseum in Amsterdam, the J. Paul Getty Museum in Los Angeles, Uffizi Gallery in Florence, the Museum of Art São Paulo in São Paulo, and National Museum of Anthropology Mexico City (among plenty of others). Today, thanks to technology, an art history class can virtually travel the world and experience, almost as if in person, the famous works that previously were only seen as thumbnail reproductions in a textbook, on slides, or through a projector.

On the other hand, modern technology allows anyone with a cell phone to record their goings-on, search online for information related to the day's lesson, and otherwise participate in education at a level never seen before. In 2018 the United States Court of Appeals for the First Circuit contemplated whether it was permissible for a student to record his classes in *Pollack v. Regional Sch. Unit 75*. Here, the parents of BP, a severely disabled, nonverbal 19-year-old public school student who was unable to communicate with his parents about his school-time experiences, requested that he use an audio recording device to record everything said in his presence during the school day. The parents wanted BP to record his day so they could review it when he came home, learn about his experiences in their absence, and advocate for him since he could not answer the question "what happened at school today" commonly asked by parents of their students. BP's school district refused the parents' request prompting them to file a suit alleging a violation of the Americans with Disabilities Act for failure to provide a reasonable accommodation.

Although the decision in *Pollock* focused more on the discrimination aspect versus the presence of personal recording devices in the classroom, the court noted district witnesses' testimony that the presence of BP's recording device would not actually support his education but, instead, would hinder it "by increasing his isolation and making staff and peers uncomfortable" (*Pollack v. Regional School Unit 75*, 2018, at 86). This begs the question—does the potential for a teacher to be filmed have a chilling effect on education? This is indeed a concern among educators, as David Strom recognized when asked about the potential for video footage of a classroom to find its way online (Honawar, 2007). Specifically, in discussing a new trend of students' videotaping teachers exhibiting all demeanors (angry, enthusiastic, silly, etc.), sometimes, over the course of many days and in some instances creating edited compilation videos of such teachers, Mr. Strom opined that this trend is "disturbing to the educational process" and could go so far as to hinder not just teachers but students from classroom participation (Honawar, 2007).

Recall the viral "no pomegranates" video (tenniscrazy, 2017) from the mid-2010s or the more recent "passionate physics professor" videos (Good Morning America, 2022). One was an example of an angry lesson (which was, in reality, a psychology lesson about teaching children with compassion rather than negativity, taken far out of context by Internet users) and the other was an example of exceptional teaching. Both videos made the Internet rounds, and both could have the same unintended consequences in terms of next-gen negligence.

Consider that the "no pomegranates" video was filmed in a high school class and is shown to a parent who asks, "What did you learn at school today?" Perhaps the parent, who only sees a brief snippet of the lesson, takes the video out of context, assuming that the teacher is being verbally abusive toward her students, and makes a complaint about the teacher to the administration. This results in the teacher being questioned about her teaching, having to defend her lesson in a situation where, had she not been videotaped, she may never have previously found herself.

While this scenario may not necessarily result in a lawsuit sounding in negligence, the simple act of videotaping the lesson may result in a chilling effect on the teacher's lesson plans going forward. Now, instead of verbally demonstrating the angry lesson and juxtaposing it with a compassionate example (which was not videotaped), perhaps the teacher simply describes the two different approaches to child-rearing, going forward. What was intended as a memorable immersive lesson has now turned into a rote lecture due to a fear of ending up as a viral Internet sensation. Being unknowingly videotaped and turning into an accidental Internet sensation is only one unintended source of next-gen negligence of which administrators need to be aware. What about people who actively seek the Internet spotlight?

With cell phones comes social media, and with social media comes influencers. In this section, we will discuss the rise of teacher-influencers. Another quick Google search for "TikTok Influencers Public School" brings up plenty of teachers with millions of views and hundreds of followers among them, sharing videos showing lesson plans and tips, setting up their classrooms, filming inside their schools, and, in the case of one PE teacher, revealing a shirtless transformation video following his fitness journey. While on its face, there may not be any harm in sharing lesson plans, tips, tricks, or advice, imagine the following scenario.

In New Jersey "instruction on the Holocaust and genocides in an appropriate place in the curriculum of all elementary and secondary school pupils" is mandated by statute (NJ Rev Stat § 18a:35-28, 2018). In accordance with these requirements, consider that a hypothetical New Jersey middle school history teacher has shared a public TikTok video explaining their lesson plans for teaching Holocaust Education to their eighth-grade class. These lesson plans include reading *Anne Frank's Diary: The Graphic Adaptation* which the teacher said in the TikTok that they included as an appropriate adaptation of Ms. Frank's famed diary for their eighth graders.

Imagine further that the TikTok video reached a middle school history teacher in Texas whose eighth-grade curriculum included the study of World War II. The Texas-based history teacher felt that including the illustrated Diary in their own lesson plans would be beneficial to their students who find history boring but love comic books. They read the book out loud to their class as part of the World War II discussions. The illustrated Diary includes drawings of Ms. Frank using the restroom, discussion of Ms. Frank having her period, of her sharing a bed with her friend Jacque, of classic nude Greek marble sculptures, and black and white swirls meant to illustrate Ms. Frank's discussion of vaginas (Goodyear, 2023). After parents learned that the Texas teacher was reading the book and showing its drawings to the class, they expressed concern to the school board which fired the teacher for negligently exposing the students to inappropriate material (inspired by Drawhorn, 2023).

Was the Texas teacher indeed negligent, though? How would your analysis change if the school had approved the lesson plans that included illustrated Diary? Do you think that the New Jersey teacher who posted the TikTok, or their administrator, could in any way be held liable for negligence in Texas? How?

Now consider the endless TikTok videos showing teachers setting up their classrooms. Many of these videos show the interior of school classrooms, where the windows and doors are, where cubbies are, how the rooms are oriented, and even the hallways leading to classrooms. "In 2022, 34 students and adults died while more than 43,000 were exposed to gunfire at school" (Sandy Hook Promise, n.d.). In a world where gun violence at schools is so prevalent, could a teacher who shared videos of their classroom setup, orientation, and location in terms of hallways, windows, potentially parking lots, and public streets as seen from the classroom interior be found negligent if a student was injured in a school shooting in their classroom? Make an argument for and against finding a teacher who had posted a classroom setup video, or their administrator's being liable for negligence in such a circumstance.

How might a high school physical education teacher with a public TikTok account on which he shares videos filmed in his gymnasium classroom related to his job as a physical education teacher and also videos from his personal life such as shirtless body transformation videos and clips of himself in swim trunks and shirtless over summer vacation open himself up to claims of negligence (inspiration for this and the following scenario are drawn from public school teacher @mr.pyper's TikTok account)?

Consider that this teacher's public TikTok account is found by some of his students who range in age from 13 (a younger freshman) to 19 (an older senior). The students watch the videos during lunchtime and get a laugh out of the teacher's silly voiceover videos and TikTok dance videos, but then they find his shirtless fitness transformation and vacation posts. The students show their parents the videos and the parents are upset that their students have now seen their teacher in a state of undress. The parents sue the school for negligence, alleging, among other claims, that the school (hence, the administrator) was negligent in failing to prevent the teacher from posting such videos publicly. Make a case for and against the administrator's liability for negligence.

Teacher-influencers are not the only way social media is an unintended source of next-gen negligence, though the examples of social media as such are far too numerous to discuss here. What other ways can we anticipate social media as a source of next-gen negligence? How do you think that these examples will play out in the court system?

Yet another unintended source of next-gen negligence is COVID-19 and the fallout that we will see as a result. Not only did COVID-19 give parents a different kind of access to their children's education than ever before, but the impact of virtual learning may yet play out on a global stage as "COVID babies" reach school age and enter the public education system.

Virtual learning opened a window to schooling through which parents could peer more closely into the classroom. Unfairly, though, this window was only a small porthole into an artificial reality, a stage set as it were. Not only were students experiencing a different mode of learning, so, too, were teachers who had never taught this way before. Additionally, teachers were tasked with providing this new kind of learning literally overnight, some asked to exit their classrooms at the end of one day, not to return for weeks or months, leaving behind their classrooms full of teaching resources with no means to access same, yet being expected to continue teaching to the same level of effectiveness as if they were in their classrooms.

This incomplete picture unquestionably revealed vulnerabilities in public education—vulnerabilities and gaps that parents, concerned about their children's well-being, were quick to identify and eager to address. That parents were also at home due to COVID-19 office closures gave them a false sense of agency based on their available time, regardless of whether they were educationally qualified to assess pedagogy and resources.

The Select Subcommittee on the Coronavirus Pandemic recently held a hearing "to examine the impact of COVID-19 closures on student development" (Committee on Oversight and Accountability, 2023). The hearing determined that "the science promoted by our federal health officers never justified the prolonged closing of schools," with one doctor, Dr. Tracy Beth Hoeg, looking to statistics from Europe showing "no relationship with the school reopening and the community case levels" and an investigative journalist, Mr. David Zweig, concluding "even if the schools were closed, over time, [the students] were going to interact with people anyway and in some cases in a more potentially dangerous fashion because you're mixing with kids from five different communities in a daycare center versus had they been in school with their own ... cohort" (Committee on Oversight and Accountability, 2023).

During the hearing, Ms. Virginia Gentles, the Director of the Education Freedom Center at the Independent Women's Forum, highlighted learning loss for students in Virginia stating:

> *Virginia schools stayed closed longer than 43 other states, resulting in devastating and widespread learning loss. The state's 13.6-point drop since 2017 in average fourth-grade National Assessment of Educational Progress (NAEP) reading scores was the largest in the nation. ... Statewide testing in 2021 revealed an 'alarming' 20-year low in early reading skills with 34.5% of K-2 students at high risk for persistent reading difficulties, in contrast to only 21.3% in 2019.* (Committee on Oversight and Accountability, 2023)

Other evidence discussed during the hearing pointed to an increase in depression, anxiety, and suicide of adolescent and young students, especially males, starting in the summer and fall of 2020, which Dr. Hoeg attributed to "social closures." Oversight Committee Chairman James Comer stated during the hearing that the public health guideline for masking children in schools was not based on science, and Dr. Hoeg confirmed that there was "evidence prior to the pandemic that masks were largely ineffective at preventing community transmission of influenza and other upper respiratory viruses" and further that "six feet of distancing was arbitrary ... based on ... how far certain sized droplets spread ... [not] on actual transmission of disease" (Committee on Oversight and Accountability, 2023).

Leaving aside, for the sake of this hypothetical discussion only, any possibility that the public schools can benefit from any tort immunity or point to government-mandated closures, how might a school be liable for negligence as it relates to choosing to COVID-19 shutdowns? Consider first a school district that closed to in-person schooling on March 11, 2020; switched to all virtual schooling one week before any government-mandated closures were enacted on March 18, 2020; remained virtual through the remainder of the 2020 school year and for the entire the 2020–2021 school year; and gave parents the option to have virtual instruction or send their children for in-person instruction beginning in Fall 2021. The schools did not prohibit virtual learning and fully reopened for in-person schooling in this hypothetical district until the 2022–2023 school year.

A seven-year-old student second-grader in this hypothetical school district during the 2019–2020 school year was forced to learn virtually from March 11, 2020, through June 2020, and for all of third grade, from September 2020 through June 2021. She finally returned to in-person instruction in September 2021, now nine years old and in the fourth grade.

Not previously diagnosed with social anxiety or disorders, the seven-year-old, once outgoing, talkative, and one who readily made new friends, returned to school withdrawn, shy, nervous, and kept going to the nurse's office with anxiety attacks experienced during recess when she had to play with other students and make friends. Her parents attributed her newfound social anxieties to her having spent formative years in quarantine, unable to attend in-person school instruction. They decide to bring a lawsuit sounding in negligence against the school district, alleging, among other things, that the school board owed a duty of care to its students to challenge the government shutdown mandates. Their failing to do so resulted in harm suffered by their daughter. Who do you think will win this lawsuit, the parents or the school board? Make an argument for and against each party. Does the administration bear any liability?

What happens when a television channel purportedly delivering news (which many people believe as true and accept at face value) is accused of defamation, a false statement purporting to be fact (Legal Information Institute, n.d.), and argues, instead, that what it airs is not actually news but "opinion commentary on matters of public importance and are not reasonably understood as being factual"? Though the case was not related to education, this is exactly the argument made by Fox News Network in the lawsuit *McDougal v. Fox News Network, LLC* in defense of its anchor Tucker Carlson's on-air statements.

The court went so far as to state that the "general tenor" of Mr. Carlson's television show should "inform a viewer that he is not 'stating actual facts' about the topics he discusses and is instead engaging in 'exaggeration' and 'non-literal commentary'" (*McDougal v. Fox News Network*, 2020). However, PBS estimates that more than three million people watch Mr. Carlson's show every night, making it the "most-watched cable *news* show" in 2021 (emphasis added) (Nawaz et al., 2022). Yet, what he is delivering is *admittedly* not (and legally determined not to be) fact—even if his viewers consider it to be. A Pew Research poll found that only 5% of Fox's viewers turn to the channel for entertainment purposes versus 44% who turn to it for the latest news and headlines (Pew Research Center Report, 2010).

This begs the question, what happens when Mr. Carlson attacks public school curricula? In 2021, Mr. Carlson's show ran a segment titled "The Far-Left Agenda Your Children Are Being Taught Every Day," during which nothing was stated making it clear that this was simply an opinion piece, despite Fox's website explicitly including the word "opinion," in the web address (Carlson, 2021). This may have been intended by Fox as an opinion piece, but with nearly half of Fox's viewers turning to the channel for news and headlines and only 5% seeking entertainment, how could a report delivered with such inflammatory language *not* affect teachers, administrators, and other public school educators? How might entertainment masquerading as news put administrators in harm's way based upon an unintended source of next-gen negligence?

The unintended source of entertainment masquerading as news goes hand in hand with another unintended source of potential administrative liability under next-gen negligence—parents taking a more active role in their students' education. Consider a hypothetical parent of a school-aged child in Buffalo, New York, who watches Tucker Carlson's television show on a nightly basis. This parent hears Mr. Carlson's (opinion) segment regarding the "far-left agenda" discussed above, during which he claims (among other things) that Buffalo's approved lesson plans include instruction on the Black Lives Matter movement (which Mr. Carlson reported is "endorsing a political movement" in a lesson plan for little kids) and are designed to imply that the nuclear family is "immoral" and that high school students in Buffalo are "being trained" to "go out into the world to destroy buildings and statues" (Carlson, 2021).

Without doing any independent research to check the validity and accuracy of Mr. Carlson's reporting (Hackford, 2020), and because the parent trusts Fox to deliver factual news and does not consider its programming to be opinion based on the network's being called Fox *News*, the parent brings a lawsuit against the Buffalo school board for negligence. In the suit, the parent alleges that the school board breached its duty not to endorse political movements, to teach family values, and to teach students to be responsible citizens who do not engage in destructive behavior. Do you think the parent would be successful in this lawsuit? Why or why not? In what other ways are parents taking a more active role in their students' education that could potentially lead to negligence claims against administrators?

What happens when students take a more active role in their own education? What if those students have differing views from their parents about what they want to learn, what is or is not appropriate to learn, and how they want to learn? What happens when kids' imaginations take over?

The Teen Prevention Education Program ("Teen PEP") is voluntary "peer-to-peer education to increase students' knowledge, attitudes, skills, and behaviors associated with healthy decision-making" (Teen PEP, n.d.), developed in 1995 and currently available in New Jersey and North Carolina. Topics explored in the Teen PEP curriculum include peer pressure, respect, sexual health, sexuality, and other sensitive topics. By using peer-to-peer education, Teen PEP students actually become the teachers—hosting events such as outreach workshops delivered by high school juniors and seniors to younger students and parents and a family night workshop "facilitated by peer educations and [providing] parents with an opportunity to dialogue with teens about sexual health issues" (Teen PEP, n.d.).

At Hunterdon Central Regional High School in Flemington, New Jersey, Liana's alma mater, Teen PEP has historically been one of the most popular health class electives—at least in the early 2000s. It was seen as an honor to be accepted into the Teen PEP class, and peers of Liana's still talk fondly about their time in the program. Teen PEP remains a popular elective, and Liana recently sat down to discuss the program with a current Teen PEP student, MM.*

On recommendation from her older sister, MM applied for Teen PEP hoping to have fun, learn in a new and exciting format, and develop good leadership skills. Although she was initially nervous to stand up and speak to younger students about potentially uncomfortable topics such as sex, sexuality, and sexual health, the idea that the Teen PEP students "take control" and have the opportunity to facilitate these important conversations was important to MM. She found that the Teen PEP class adequately addressed the awkwardness that surrounds such topics by diffusing the situation with skits that break the tension and allow students to feel comfortable asking questions and exploring topics they "would not necessarily feel comfortable discussing with their parents" (MM, personal communication, November 15, 2023).

Interestingly, MM emphasized how important she feels it is for younger students to have truth and accuracy in their education. MM explained, "When you are in high school, you are mature enough to talk about complex things like sex, healthy relationships, and drug use," and feels that students should be trusted to explore these topics in ways not only that provide them with an accurate information regarding same, but that it would do a disservice to their education to opt out of learning about such topics, especially at the high school age, where they face entering the "real world" (whether that be an immediate entry into the workforce or by leaving home for college) in just a few short years. Specifically, MM felt that "while most people know how things work, many don't—and if they do not have access to accurate information about real life issues, they could find themselves in bad or sticky situations that could have easily been avoided—and Teen PEP allows students not only to learn about these real life issues, but also gives us the opportunity to make sure our peers also have this important information."

Although MM has a vehicle to take control of her education directly through her involvement in Teen PEP, she is a shining example of students taking control of their education, and speaking out about what they want to learn and how they want to learn it. MM is certainly not the only student who wants to take an active role in her education, whether that be through selecting electives that fit their interests, enrolling in classes such as Teen PEP, protesting book bans, or otherwise advocating for learning what is important to them.

But, let's consider what would have happened if a student interested in taking Teen PEP, who needs a signed permission slip to enroll in Teen PEP. Her parent does not want her to learn from a sex ed curriculum in school and refuses to sign the permission slip. This student goes to her guidance counselor and asks to be waived in, despite the lack of permission slip. Thus, she is enrolled in the class, despite her parent's wishes for her not to be. Could the parent bring a claim of negligence against the school? What about the opposite—what if the parent completely opted the student out of not just Teen PEP, but health class, entirely, and the student never learned about sex, sexual health, or other topics taught in health classes, remaining completely ignorant of these topics. If the student contracts an STD, could the student bring a claim for negligence against the school for their failure to admit them into a Teen PEP or other health class?

Let's now consider this scenario as we think about how imaginative play can be an unintended source of next-gen negligence. A kindergarten class is made up of about 15 students, all of whom are incredibly close friends who socialize not only during school but frequently during non-school hours. Their parents are all friendly; the students often have play dates with each other, and they are all included in each other's birthday parties.

The entire class plays together during recess, and one day they decide to play "house," assigning each person a role. On Monday, Sally and Tom are cast as "mom" and "dad," respectively, and Anne is cast as their daughter. They go home after school and tell their parents about their new game, to which no parent objects. On Tuesday, Anne and Sally decide that they want to be married that day because they are best friends with Tom as their son. The teacher observes them playing house on Monday and Tuesday and does not step in either day to encourage the students to take on different roles or voice any objection to Anne and Sally being "married."

When Sally goes home on Tuesday, she tells her mom she was not married to Tom anymore but instead married Anne because they are best friends. Sally's mom is enraged and tells Anne that she cannot be married to Sally anymore during the game because "girls cannot marry other girls!" On Wednesday during recess, Sally tells Anne she cannot marry her today because girls cannot marry other girls, so, instead, Sally and Anne decide to role-play as sisters. Anne is confused and sad that her best friend Sally does not want to marry her anymore, and when she goes home, she tells her mom what happened at school. Anne's mom gives her a hug and says that "anyone can marry anyone as long as they love each other and treat each other with kindness."

Thursday at recess, Anne tells Sally "Good news! We can be married today because my mom said anyone can marry anyone if they love each other and are nice to each other!" The girls happily play "married" on Thursday, and when Sally gets home, she tells her mom about being married to Anne again. Sally's mom is furious and calls Anne's mom to yell at her for "pushing" her liberal agenda on Sally. Is there negligence here? By whom? Should the teacher have intervened when she saw Sally and Anne playing married on Tuesday? What about on Thursday? What if on Tuesday, instead of just telling Sally she did not want her pretending to marry Anne, Sally's mother had also sent an email telling the principal about this game? Could the teacher be negligent then for letting the two girls role-play in this manner? How could this situation have been avoided?

More importantly, *should* public school administrators seek to prevent this type of role-playing in their classrooms? How much can and should schools have control over the lives of their students while at school? What are the limits to *in loco parentis* that might help to define an administrator's liability for negligence from unexpected sources?

An answer may lie in a case from the 1800s that has recently been cited by the U.S. Supreme Court in *Mahanoy Area School District v. B.L.* (see Chap. 8). This 1859 case from Vermont, *Lander v. Seaver*, addresses the issue of *in loco parentis*, adding definition to the roles of, at the time, the schoolmaster and the parent. In *Lander*, the court's concern was discipline of a student off school grounds, and that was the connection made to the 2023 issue in *Mahanoy*. However, the opinion of the *Lander* court potentially reaches many aspects of the respective roles of school and home. Judge Asa Aldis, the author of this opinion, distinguishing between the roles of parent and school writes:

> [The schoolmaster] *may not safely be trusted with all a parent's authority, for he does not act from the instinct of parental affection. He should be guided and restrained by judgment and wise discretion, and hence is responsible for their reasonable exercise.* (*Lander v. Seaver*, 1859, at 122–123)

He goes on to cite Judge Michael Blackstone in defining *in loco parentis*, saying:

> '*The [school]master is in* loco parentis, *and has such a*, portion *of the powers of the parent committed to his charge, as may be necessary to answer the purposes for which he is employed.' An English annotator, in a note to the passage, very properly adds, 'this power must be temperately exercised, and no schoolmaster should feel himself at liberty to administer chastisement coextensive with the parent.'* (*Lander v. Seaver*, 1859, at 123)

Judge Aldis provides among the most specific guidance defining the parameters within which an administrator must act as regards their duties to their students. He cites an 1855 Massachusetts case, *Commonwealth v. Randall* in saying:

> *[T]he schoolmaster is liable only When he acts* malo animo, *from vindictive feelings, or under the violent impulses of passion or malevolence, and that he is not liable for errors of opinion or mistakes of judgment, provided he is governed by an honest purpose of heart, to promote by the discipline employed, the highest welfare of the school and the best interest of the scholar.* (*Lander v. Seaver*, 1859, at 123)

This may be something on which administrators can hang their hats if accused of negligence, especially from unexpected sources—and especially from those lacking precedent.
*Informed consent to participate and to publish was obtained from MM's parent.

REFERENCES

Carlson, T. (2021, February 19). *The far-left agenda your children are being taught every day.* Fox News Media. https://www.foxnews.com/opinion/tucker-carlson-far-left-agenda-schools-blm

Committee on Oversight and Accountability. (2023, March 29). *School closures hearing wrap-up: Preparing our education system to address a future pandemic starts with holding ourselves and our agencies accountable.* U.S. House of Representatives. https://oversight.house.gov/release/school-closures-hearing-wrap-up-preparing-our-education-system-to-address-a-future-pandemic-starts-with-holding-ourselves-and-our-agencies-accountable%EF%BF%BC/

Drawhorn, A. (2023, September 13). *Controversy over the graphic adaptation of the "Diary of Anne Frank" prompts the ousting of an H-F ISD teacher.* CBS 6KFDM. https://kfdm.com/news/local/investigation-underway-after-hamshire-fannett-students-read-sexual-content-in-anne-frank-diary

Good Morning America. (2022). Passionate professor's physics demonstrations go viral. YouTube. https://youtu.be/6evA9V-U3Ec?si=j4j1UZ1ua3nyTuAl

Goodyear, S. (2023, September 22). *Illustrator stands by graphic novel of Anne Frank's diary that got Texas teacher fired.* CBC Radio. https://www.cbc.ca/radio/asithappens/anne-frank-graphic-novel-controversy-1.6975989#:~:text=In%20April%2C%20a%20Florida%20high,school%20district's%20libraries%20in%20August

Hackford, R. (2020, September 18). *New Buffalo public schools curriculum receives national attention.* 2WGRZ. https://www.wgrz.com/article/news/education/new-buffalo-public-schools-curriculum-receives-national-attention/71-992b3715-d899-4cf8-a659-f1255d39f113

Honawar, V. (2007, November 5). Cellphones in classrooms land teachers on online video sites. *Education Week.* https://www.edweek.org/technology/cellphones-in-classrooms-land-teachers-on-online-video-sites/2007/11

Lander v. Seaver, 32 Vt. 114(1859).

Legal Information Institute. (n.d.). Defamation. https://www.law.cornell.edu/wex/defamation

McDougal v. Fox News Network, LLC, 489 F. Supp. 3d 174 (S.D.N.Y. 2020).

Nawaz, A., Loffman, M., & Evans, T. (2022, May 2). *Tucker Carlson's influence and his increasingly extreme views.* PBS News Hour. https://www.pbs.org/

newshour/show/tucker-carlsons-influence-and-his-increasingly-extreme-views
NJ Rev Stat § 18a:35-28 (2018).
Pew Research Center Report. (2010, September 12). *Section 4: Who is listening, watching, reading–and why.* Pew Research Center. https://www.pewresearch.org/politics/2010/09/12/section-4-who-is-listening-watching-reading-and-why/
Pollack v Regional School Unit 75, 886 F3d 75 (1st Cir. 2018).
Sandy Hook Promise. (n.d.). *17 facts about gun violence and school shootings.* Sandyhookpromise.org. https://www.sandyhookpromise.org/blog/gun-violence/facts-about-gun-violence-and-school-shootings/
Teen PEP. (n.d.). *Teen Prevention Education Program.* Supportive Schools. https://www.supportiveschools.org/teen-pep
tenniscrazy908. (2017). Class teacher no pomegranates. YouTube. https://youtu.be/A91F0wOOehQ?si=m1exqHjBzrUwzsT0

PART V

Next-Gen Negligence Going Forward

CHAPTER 15

Next-Gen Negligence and the Future of Public Education

Abstract Chapter 15 explores two looming frontiers for public education: artificial intelligence (AI) and what the future will look like for schooling. Drawing from reflections on the 1980s emergence of computer technology in schools as well as current perceptions of the cautionary use of AI in education today, the authors speak to the need for dialogue and training to best prepare for the unknown. This theme continues through the authors' discussion of how education is likely to change in the future to adapt to a world very different from that which public education was first developed to serve.

Keywords Artificial intelligence • ChatGPT • Privacy • Internet use policies • Technology • Future • Futurists • Workplace/workforce

Next-gen negligence has significant meaning when considering the complex and somewhat tenuous future of public education as we currently and traditionally have known it. Although there are many areas that could be explored, we have selected two that are notable because they are still, at this point, relative unknowns—blank slates as it were for determining responsibility and even how they fit into public education. There is no doubt that artificial intelligence (AI) and the study of futuristics as related to education will impact schooling and take an administrator's responsibilities relative to duty and negligence to levels yet unexperienced. When and how remain to be seen!

Artificial Intelligence (AI)

While any number of articles are currently being written about projections for AI and its use in education, President Biden's Executive Order "seiz[ing] the promise and manag[ing] the risks of artificial intelligence" (FACT SHEET, 2023) is particularly relevant for administrators and the potential for liability under next-gen negligence.

Of importance in the public education setting, the President's executive order "calls on Congress to pass bipartisan data privacy legislation to protect all Americans, especially kids" (FACT SHEET, 2023). This Fact Sheet and another White House document, entitled the *Blueprint for an AI Bill of Rights* (n.d.) speak to ensuring the privacy of student and staff information; the use or misuse of data that classifies students and staff in ways that potentially compromise their right to Equal Protection under the Fourteenth Amendment; and the future transformation of education into models for schooling the extent of which we cannot yet clearly define. In next-gen negligence terms, duties and injuries may look the same, but administrators will need to be aware of a wider variety of ways to meet those duties and anticipate those injuries with an obligation to secure privileged information and make available equitable learning opportunities.

ChatGPT is one of the more immediate AI challenges facing administrators. ChatGPT brings the potential for negligence, particularly in terms of an administrator's need to oversee and maintain curriculum integrity. Concerns abound regarding the potential for students to substitute computer-generated work for their own, as well as for teachers being able to identify abuses of the technology and receive proper training in its use. Consider the following scenario:

A high school student must write a research paper. Although the student performs all of the research themselves, they use AI to generate their citations and reference list at the end of the paper. The student turns the paper in; the teacher does not realize that AI was used to generate the citations and reference list and awards a passing grade.

The student passes the class and next semester again has to write another research paper, this time for a different teacher in a different class and subject entirely. For this assignment, the student again relies on AI to generate their citations and reference list. Now, however, the teacher discovers that the student has used AI to complete the assignment, awards a failing grade, and refers the student for further, more serious disciplinary action.

Although the school has anti-cheating and anti-plagiarism policies in place, the school has not explicitly included any discussion of the use of AI in either of these policies. Does this student have a viable negligence claim against the first teacher for failing to teach them how to write a citation/reference list without relying on AI or for the administrator for not ensuring that AI-related instruction is included in the curriculum? What about failing to catch them using AI in the first place? Imagine that a suit is actually brought against the school and administration. What are the defenses against negligence the school could argue?

Students' opinions about what schools should do regarding ChatGPT reveal two recommendations:

1. *Implement better guidelines, suggestions and protocols on how to use ChatGPT.*
2. *Teach students how to use ChatGPT to advance academic skills.* (Coleman et al., 2023, p. 30)

To safeguard students' privacy and make parents aware when schools employ ChatGPT or AI in general, some schools have taken to using permission slips, similar to those issued for field trips or sensitive subject matter or simply notifying parents at the start of the school year that students may be using AI in their learning. While this doesn't protect against data collection from outside sources, informing parents brings them into the conversation—to learn about AI and how it is being used in schools (Klein, 2023).

Klein goes on to share other cautionary advice that would be helpful in limiting administrators' liability for negligence in this area. First, it is important to check privacy guidelines for any tool used that has the potential to collect data. While administrators may not be the ones directly supervising students' use of the technology, they bear overall responsibility for student safety—which includes safeguarding student data and access to information on the Internet. Klein goes on to quote Amelia Vance, president of the Public Interest Privacy Center, who advises that students should be directed not to share personal information when using applications such as ChatGPT and to "'turn off their history,' a feature ChatGPT added … that allows users to ask questions without the conversation being later used as training data for the tool'" (Klein, 2023). These suggestions are ideal for administrators to include in district Internet use policies.

We began Chap. 12 with a reference to Beth's own dissertation, a ground-breaking study from the 1980s, a time when few schools and even fewer administrators were likely considering the intrusion of technology into traditional schooling. Today, as the future of public education grows even more connected to AI, administrators must be attuned to what is coming so as not to be liable for next-gen negligence.

Beth's recommendations as the result of her research are interesting when considering next-gen negligence vis-à-vis AI and the future of public education. Consider that these recommendations were made in the 1980s pertaining to computer use in education, perhaps one of the earliest inflection points for technology in formal schooling (Inflection point, n.d.). As regards AI, education, and, indeed, our world, is clearly at another moment when significant change has occurred. Beth recommended:

- First, dialogue takes place between experts in the field and educators so that ideas might be shared and goals jointly developed for implementing computer technology in education.
- Next, there be more opportunities for the computer to be used in the research phase of education as a retrieval mechanism for students and teachers.
- Third, teachers need training in computer literacy, curriculum applications of computer technology, and software evaluation and development.
- Fourth, educators need to be incentivized so that they are aware of and have the support of their administration to advance technology use in education.
- Fifth, those creating software connect with educators for the purpose of understanding the applications of technology in schools. And, finally, an administrative position should be created in school districts to address technology needs (Godett, 1986, pp. 170–172).

Each of these five recommendations can translate to apply to the advent of AI. Consider them with respect to the scenario mentioned earlier about the student writing a research paper and regarding the use of AI with the generation of citations and reference pages. How would each recommendation factor in? How do you see each of these recommendations being considered by the courts in a next-gen negligence case?

The importance of dialogue, planning, maximization of potential resources, training, support, and management continue to be critical considerations, as they were when computer technology first emerged on the education scene in the late 1970s and 1980s. The challenge for administrators going forward is to be able to anticipate needs for horizon technologies of which we are yet unaware that may appear in the hands of children long before they enter the schools.

Defining the Workplace/Workforce of the Future

Shaping the future of public schooling has recently taken center stage as state legislators have taken steps to restrict what may be taught in K-12 public school classrooms and activism on the part of vocal stakeholders has confounded established and long-recognized educator roles. Newly enacted laws appear to be forcing some to rethink their careers and the districts/states in which they serve. This becomes a twofold issue as administrators struggle to staff their schools with talented teachers and address their duty to provide a constitutionally guaranteed level of educational opportunities for all children—all while complying with state-imposed laws. Not only is this concerning to the daily functioning of public schools, but it threatens the profession's ability to create a future for students in sync with a technologically evolving society.

Legislation where the state has assumed the responsibility for defining what and how teachers can teach, especially since 2021, has had a tremendous impact on teachers' agency in their profession. Key findings from the Rand Corporation's 2022 American Instructional Resources Survey reveal that, of those surveyed,

- *Roughly one-quarter of teachers reported not knowing whether they were subject to restrictions on how they can address topics related to race or gender, and only 30 percent of teachers in states with restrictions reported them as being in place.*

- *Restrictions infringed on teachers' autonomy by constraining the topics they could address and their choice of instructional materials and discussion topics.*
- *Teachers perceived that limitations placed on how they can address race- or gender-related topics negatively affected their working conditions, and they worried about limitations' consequences for student learning.* (Woo et al., 2022)

Recommendations from this study speak not only to state officials, but also to those in school governance and administration. They include:

- the need to collaborate with teachers to create "local policies and guidance and integrate their perspectives and concerns to ensure the health and diversity of the workforce";
- the need to "provide teachers with the appropriate guidance, resources, and supports to address contentious topics in the classroom and message their support for teachers";
- the need to "strive to engage families in productive conversations about race and gender"; and
- the need to "tie potentially contentious topics to create learning objectives and emphasize their educational benefits for students" (Woo et al., 2022).

Here is yet another opportunity to look back at Beth's recommendations from the 1980s as they connect with the duties of administrators today. Making connections, learning from one another, communicating expectations, and providing support may be what are needed to create greater awareness of educators' expertise in creating curricula and programs. That may also help reestablish a focus on students that is falling victim to legislative blindness today.

Administrators' duties to students and staff include helping forge a new path forward, even though it may be easier to tacitly walk the state line. That silence can be viewed as a form of deliberate indifference akin to an administrator's knowing something exists as a problem and failing to take action to improve the situation. In a world where politics invades school board governance and usurps district control over curriculum development and pedagogy, administrators cannot surrender control over how the learning needs of students are met.

This may be easy to say; however, administrators' ability to maintain control over what public schooling can provide is more complicated than it appears. Administrators are up against certain realities that are in motion more rapidly now than ever.

In addition to challenges related to governance, public school enrollment is declining, and districts are facing the need to close schools. District leadership has had to contend with what *Education Week*'s Caitlynn Peetz reports as rapidly declining birth rates, families choosing options to public education, population shifts away from urban settings, and the expiration of relief funding provided during the COVID-19 pandemic that will expire later in 2024. Peetz quotes David DeSchryver of Whiteboard Advisors, a communications, research, and consulting firm saying, "Those factors have merged to create the 'perfect storm' for many districts' enrollments and budgets, leading more to put school building closures on the table" (Peetz, 2024). Diminishing budgets and facilities puts a strain on school administrators' abilities to fulfill their duty to provide students with the learning opportunities assured by state constitutions.

Abbie Cohen in the *Kappan* posits that it may be true that public schools are no longer able to address student needs because of "Americans' differing visions about what purpose schools are supposed to serve." These differing visions, according to Cohen, create tension between public schools as serving "a public good" with the perception that schools are a "private commodity, treat[ing] families as consumers" (Cohen, 2023, n.p.). And these differing views of what a public school is supposed to do result in emerging and (depending upon where one lives) surging alternatives for learning, including homeschooling and private school options that pull funding from public education.

So where does this leave administrators, really?

Daniel Susskind is an economist known for his TED talks and writings on the impact AI could have on the future of work, society, and education. If one pays attention to what Susskind shares in his book, *A World Without Work*, as well as to the theories of education futurists, there is potential for an administrative role that may force the hand of legislators and those seeking to insert their own agendas on how not only their children but the children *of others* are taught. These insights speak to an enhanced sense of those to whom a duty is owed, as well as an energized scope of those duties.

Simply put, what Susskind and education futurists tell us is that with increasing automation, schooling will need to change. The parental power borne of fear that public education will expose children to a world inconsistent with their beliefs may not be sustainable when technology outpaces schooling as we know it. Susskind suggests that we need to begin thinking about how we educate young people and ways to do that differently by looking at "what we teach, how we teach it, and when we teach it" (Susskind, 2022, p. 155).

The scope of an administrator's duty to provide a curriculum that meets the needs of students is changing. On the one hand, Holly Spanner of the BBC's *Science Focus* speaks of schooling as "largely unchanged for the past 100 or so years—pupils are divided by age and the curriculum broken down into subjects." She admits that schooling "has been adapted to incorporate new technologies, as well as responding to economic, social, and political changes," and does not offer hope for drastic change within the next several decades. However, she does expect schooling will "*adapt* to our evolving world" and reveal changes in the way we access information and use technology to collect and use data and facilitate learning (Spanner, 2023).

Bernard Marr, writing for *Forbes* notes, "Our world is changing fast. The pace of change, particularly when it comes to new technologies, means the half-life of skills is shrinking fast. ... The education sector must adapt in line with this shift and reflect the fact that the essential, in-demand skills of the future will be very different from what has been taught in the past. ... [W]hat we teach has to change." Marr speaks of teachers becoming "*facilitators* rather than content deliverers" and learning that is online with digitized content, "personalized, self-paced, and self-directed ... collaborative project-based ... and bite-sized" (Marr, 2022).

GoStudent, a worldwide provider of tutoring, sees schooling over the next 25 years as undergoing tremendous change, leaving behind traditional images of classroom learning. The organization's report, *Revolutionising Education*, speaks to completely digitized education that is "skill-based rather than age-related" with "AI technology [providing] instant in-person translation, meaning students of many different nationalities can learn together" (GoStudent, 2023). Imagine how this idea of truly lifelong learning would expand the idea of to whom a duty is owed!

GoStudent's founder, Felix Ohswald comments, "'Education is at an inflexion point'.... To actively continue to shape the future of how students learn we must embrace what lies ahead" (GoStudent, 2023). The organization's futurists speak to classrooms exceeding their physical confines, learning as immersive and personal, and the need to rise to meet new technologies and AI. In contrast to *Forbes*' Marr, GoStudent's Tracey Follows sees the educators' role as moving *away* from that of facilitator and toward personal coaching with the classroom "distributed across the learners' lives" with knowledge "instantly available via virtual training spaces for whatever, whenever and wherever someone would like to learn" (Follows, 2023, p. 5). Again, consider how this could monumentally change the role and responsibilities of a public school administrator—especially in terms of control over curriculum and the identification and provision of teaching and support staff!

Susskind's perspective has parallels to what we learn from some futurists. "How we teach," according to Susskind, involves entering more virtual learning spaces to maximize outreach as "teaching in a classroom is unavoidably 'one size fits all.' Teachers cannot tailor their materials to the specific needs of every student" resulting in education that is "one size fits none" (Susskind, 2022, p. 159).

At the present time, it would be a tremendous task to effectively implement the vision of futurists in fulfillment of administrators' duties to provide students with challenging learning opportunities. It would also be a hard sell to the public in the recent aftermath of virtual learning during COVID-19 pandemic school closures. Giving thought to the ideas of education futurists, though, may help administrators and public education governing boards identify the curricula and pedagogy of the future, as well as options for schooling less confined to a limited set of resources and learning environments. Consider how engaging in this work that redefines learning could be game-changing for administrators! Think back to Beth's dissertation recommendations clearing a place to engage the "experts" of this new future—both those with the technological know-how and those who understand pedagogy.

The ideas brought by education seers open up new possibilities for enhancing administrative duty in a positive way—in a direction that speaks of promise rather than the inevitability of limitations. It is hardly far-fetched to contemplate administrators partnering with their students to craft a future for public education!

Indeed, futurist Arthur Shostak's prescient 2008 study, *Anticipate the School You Want: Futurizing K-12 Education*, suggests creating a Futures Committee composed of school stakeholder recruits. He notes "a futurizing campaign is beyond the capacity of any one of us," and what he calls a diverse "band of kindred souls, a sparkling cadre … of enthusiastic first-responders" is necessary to engage stakeholders in how they "imagine attention to the future might improve K-12 schooling in general and [their] school in particular." Shostak speaks of the need for "attractive images of the future, rather than ... staid analysis" (Shostak, 2008, pp. 36, 40).

As Follows notes in her GoStudent white paper, learning is destined to become omnipresent. This, along with Susskind's "when we teach," is a goal administrators will need to address in fulfilling their duty to both their students and their stakeholders. What we learn from futurists helps us understand that traditional brick-and-mortar education will ultimately give way to learning that engages potentially all stakeholders throughout their lives.

While the administrator's duty could become daunting as it exponentially grows, the future affords opportunities for administrators to have more agency and to *give* more agency to teachers and students alike. Shostak illustrates this by quoting Marcus Bussey, seeing the future as a "spreading 'web' or 'tree' of alternative possibilities growing out of the present" (Shostak, 2008, p. 17). Sharing the responsibility for learning can position administrators for success rather than put them on the defensive. In Susskind's words, "embracing lifelong learning is a way of insuring ourselves against the unknowable demands that the working world of the future might make on us" (Susskind, 2022, p. 161).

Linda Darling-Hammond, in a 2022 article in the *Kappan*, speaks to how education has changed and what is needed for the future. She crystallizes the impression and reality of education's history as that of "sorting students," "maximiz[ing] role learning and rule-following and minimiz[ing] the cultivation of personal interests and relationships" (Darling-Hammond, 2022). However, she also speaks to the potential for reinvention because of how our society has progressed scientifically and in its understanding of human development. She notes,

> *[W]e need to undo many of the policies that prop up the existing model and replace them with ones that encourage us to enact the kinds of curricular designs, learning communities, high-quality assessments, community partnerships, and teaching practices that my fellow contributors to this series have described.* (Darling-Hammond, 2022)

To wit, she calls for funding and designing schools so they are able to support deeper learning and equity for all students and foster the building of relationships. She also speaks to the importance of reconsidering how we prepare those who teach, including licensing and opportunities for sustained professional development.

Education has never been an institution known for its resilience or for its capacity to mobilize quickly in the face of change. Safeguarding against any administrator's liability for negligence will mean developing clear definitions of not only those to whom a duty is owed and the scope of those duties but also what injury will look like in a world of enhanced technology and automation. It will require administrators to engage their curiosity about the future and to anticipate how public education can be more readily adaptable to change that is neither predictable nor within its control.

Education is faced with the proverbial problem of building the plane while flying it. This makes liability for negligence on the part of public school administrators a moving target, difficult to picture clearly and even harder to address. Even as our country appears to be mired in ideological battles between reason and power, there are glimmers of hope as courage begins to overtake fear when it comes to electing those who can move education forward. Whether or not some wish to go there, the plane we are building while in flight is, in reality, a spaceship hurtling toward points unknown!

REFERENCES

Blueprint for an AI bill of rights. (n.d.). The White House. https://www.whitehouse.gov/ostp/ai-bill-of-rights/#discrimination

Cohen, A. (2023, January 30). The forces underlying the public school enrollment drop. *Kappan*. https://kappanonline.org/public-school-enrollment-drop-cohen/

Coleman, G., Roth, N., Iturrate, I., & Klein, T. (2023, November). AI in the classroom? *New Jersey Education Association Review*.

Darling-Hammond, L. (2022, May). Possible futures: The policy changes we need to get there. *Kappan*. https://kappanonline.org/possible-futures-policy-changes-darling-hammond/

FACT SHEET: President Biden issues executive order on safe, secure, and trustworthy artificial intelligence. (2023, October 30). The White House. https://www.whitehouse.gov/briefing-room/statements-releases/2023/10/30/fact-sheet-president-biden-issues-executive-order-on-safe-secure-and-trustworthy-artificial-intelligence/

Follows, T. (2023). *The end of school as you know it: Education in 2050.* GoStudent. https://hello1.gostudent.org/en/education-in-2050/?_gl=1*11fufhl*_ga*MjAyNzYwNzQzOS4xNzA0ODA1MDYw*_ga_LSGQLNQFS9*MTcwNDgwNTA2MC4xLjAuMTcwNDgwNTA2MC4wLjAuMA

Godett, B. (1986). *Computer use in education: From goals to realities.* (Unpublished doctoral dissertation). Lehigh University.

GoStudent. (2023, September 4). *Revolutionising education: A glimpse into the future of education in 2050.* GoStudent. https://www.gostudent.org/en/press-releases/revolutionising-education:-a-glimpse-into-the-future-of-education-in-2050

Inflection point. (n.d.). *Merriam-Webster.com dictionary.* Merriam-Webster. https://www.merriam-webster.com/dictionary/inflection%20point

Klein, A. (2023, November 7). Permission slips to use ChatGPT? Some schools say they're necessary. *Education Week.* https://www.edweek.org/technology/permission-slips-to-use-chatgpt-some-schools-say-theyre-necessary/2023/11

Marr, B. (2022, January 21). The 2 biggest future trends in education. *Forbes.* https://www.forbes.com/sites/bernardmarr/2022/01/21/the-2-biggest-future-trends-in-education/?sh=3c0af0de2d6f

Peetz, C. (2024, January 8). As enrollment declines, districts consider closing schools. *Education Week.* https://www.edweek.org/leadership/as-enrollment-declines-districts-consider-closing-schools/2024/01

Shostak, A. (2008). *Anticipate the school you want.* Rowman & Littlefield Education.

Spanner, H. (2023, January 31). *What could the school of 2050 look like?* BBC Science Focus. https://www.sciencefocus.com/future-technology/the-school-of-2050-technology-education

Susskind, D. (2022). *A world without work: Technology, automation, and how we should respond.* Picador.

Woo, A., Lee, S., Tuma, A.P., Kaufman, J., Lawrence, R.A., & Reed, N. (2022). *Walking on eggshells—Teachers' responses to classroom limitations on race- or gender-related topics.* The Rand Corporation. https://www.rand.org/pubs/research_reports/RRA134-16.html.

CHAPTER 16

Postscript: Another Note from the Authors

Abstract This final chapter helps readers to draw conclusions using assumptions, aha moments, and take-aways. It is intended to bring closure while, at the same time, prompting and promoting administrators to ponder schooling's connections to the greater world and society. The authors have provided a forum within which administrators may consider the law relative to realistic scenarios. It is hoped that such consideration will lead school leaders to decision-making based first on the law, but also on curiosity, an expansive thirst for knowledge, and hope for the future.

Keywords Assumptions • Aha! considerations • Take-aways • Teacher rights

Dear Reader,

This marks the end of our journey together exploring next-gen negligence and the potential for administrative liability—at least for now! As you can tell from our discussions, our case stories, our hypothetical scenarios, and our probing questions, not only is this a topic we could easily continue exploring with its present-day applications, but it is one that is also constantly unfolding. We leave you now with a series of basic

© The Author(s), under exclusive license to Springer Nature
Switzerland AG 2024
B. Godett, L. M. Nobile, *Exploring Administrative Decision-Making in Public Education*,
https://doi.org/10.1007/978-3-031-58782-5_16

assumptions to guide your current practice, Aha! considerations that may not have crossed your mind but that could become even more influential in the future, and take-aways to think about for your practice yet to come.

Basic assumption #1: Anyone can file suit at any time for any reason, whether or not the claims are thought to be meritorious. It is also difficult to predict how any case will play out in court because cases related to negligence are likely fact-sensitive inquiries, meaning there won't be summary judgment decisions. It is most likely that until there is good case law out there to give us guidance, these cases will have to go to a jury, and the way any case ends up could easily vary from jurisdiction to jurisdiction (e.g., a case sounding in next-gen negligence in a state like Florida could likely look very different than a case in a state like California or Vermont).

Basic assumption #2: The four essential elements of classic negligence remain the four essential elements of what we have discussed as next-gen negligence.

Aha! #1: State constitutions carry great authority. They have the potential to establish—and, in some cases, have established education as a "fundamental right," something to this point denied by the U.S. Constitution (Brennan-Gac, 2014).

Aha! #2: The idea of a "duty" can be coexistent with what may be considered as a "right."

Aha! #3: Consider the possibility that a student's right to education as guaranteed under their state's constitution can also imply a teacher's right to teach—and what this means for an administrator's duty. Joshua E. Weishart, in his law review article "The Right to Teach," takes the position that "state actors may not compel teaching practices inconsistent with the state constitutional duty to educate democratically in the classroom" (Weishart, 2022, p. 818). Perhaps broadening the element of duty, Weishart speaks of the right to education as something "different constitutional stakeholders hold … concurrently" (Weishart, 2022, p. 869). He outlines the duty implicated by this right as "an affirmative duty on the state to provide a constitutionally adequate and equitable education and … freedom from inadequate and inequitable educational opportunities of which the state is responsible" (Weishart, 2022, p. 869)—a right with an accompanying duty to students.

Of parents and guardians, he notes that their stake in a right to education "takes the sole form of a privilege, conferring the freedom 'to elect a public or private education for their children and to maintain some degree of control over their children's education'" (Weishart, 2022, p. 869). This helps to define a parent's role that seemingly separates it from the idea that parental voice generates an administrative duty.

A teacher's right and the administrator's corresponding duty are perhaps best articulated in Weishart's conclusion to his research that comes with an imperative to administrators. He says, "It is difficult to imagine a bright future for America's public school teachers until, at the very least, we recognize teacher rights as education rights **and protect teachers as professional educators**" (emphasis added) (Weishart, 2022, p. 886).

Take-away #1: Negligence exists in partnership with any of a number of possible accusations of wrongdoing including constitutional violations and/or inadequate provisions of entitlements. It is not something you can expect to see by itself.

Take-away #2: The most likely differences between classic negligence and next-gen negligence are an expansion of those to whom an administrator may owe a duty, the evolution of new duties, and the scope of injuries that may be suffered as a result of a breach.

Take-away #3: When considering next-gen negligence going forward, look at the case of *Peter W.* with reference to public policy in all its glory. Virtual schooling during and after COVID-19 endowed the public with a voice and the confidence to use it regarding public education to a greater extent than ever before. The guidelines from *Peter W.* can provide an understanding of what public policy is to help administrators deal with the impact it can have.

Take-away #4: Never accept that a case decided, especially by the U.S. Supreme Court, seeming to have nothing to do with education, actually doesn't have anything to do with education. One important illustration of this is the Supreme Court's recent ruling in *Dobbs v. Jackson* (2022) which overturned *Roe v. Wade* (1973). Although, like *Roe, Dobbs* was about abortion and women's rights to make decisions about their own bodies and health, Raquel Muñiz in her essay, "The Need for Educational Research Engagement with Courts, Public Policy, and Practice in a Post-*Dobbs* Era," speaks to *Dobbs* in terms of its impact on "reproductive justice" or "the ability to make choices about one's own body" (Muñiz, 2023, p. 1).

She notes how rulings such as the one in *Dobbs* can have a direct impact on education saying how this ruling, and the state legislation that has followed, "target K-12 curricula, prohibiting or restricting discussions of gender, gender identity, and sexuality" (Muñiz, 2023, p. 1, quoting Lewis et al., 2023). She also sees a connection between legislative restrictions and the ability of "marginalized students who can carry pregnancies [and] are unable to fully engage in their education because social policies and educational structures fail to support them pre- and postpartum" (Muñiz, 2023, p. 2). Muñiz notes that schools "play an important role in promoting bodily autonomy" through their K-12 health curriculum that includes instruction related to "reproductive systems and healthy relationships" (Muñiz, 2023, p. 2). There are many other ways administrators may envision the fallout from restrictive state legislation such as that coming from *Dobbs* that impact the rights of those to whom they owe a duty in their roles.

Take-away #5: Seek out and embrace the inflection points in education and in our world. They will help you stay attuned to expectations and realities that may impact your administrative responsibilities—and perceptions of those responsibilities!

We are hoping that you will agree that our assumptions, Ahas!, and take-aways serve to bring our work full circle, tying up the points we have endeavored to make by looking at an administrator's liability for negligence through a new and perhaps more focused lens. Just like so much else in the law, there are no absolute answers just as there are no guarantees. There will always be legal risks, both known and unknown, ancillary to an administrator's professional responsibilities.

Our goal in offering our work to you, dear reader, has been to help you identify issues over which you may have control before they become legal issues over which you may not. We hope you will benefit from reading and that you will share and recommend our work to your colleagues!

Beth and Liana

REFERENCES

Brennan-Gac, T. (2014, April 1). *Educational rights in the states.* American Bar Association. https://www.americanbar.org/groups/crsj/publications/human_rights_magazine_home/2014_vol_40/vol_40_no_2_civil_rights/educational_rights_states/

Muñiz, R. (2023, October 6). The need for educational research engagement with courts, public policy, and practice in a post-*Dobbs* era. *Educational Researcher,* XX(X), 1–7.

Weishart, J.E. (2022). The right to teach. *U.C. Davis Law Review,* 56(817). https://lawreview.law.ucdavis.edu/issues/56/2/articles/files/56-2_Weishart.pdf

Case Index

A

A.C. v. Raimondo, 494 F. Supp. 3d 170 (D.R.I. 2020), 32–34, 94, 95

Alexander v. Yale University, 631 F.2d 178 (2d Cir. 1980), 89

Armijo v. Wagon Mound Public Schools, 159 F.3d 1253 (10th Cir. 1998), 110

B

Bethel School District No. 403 v. Fraser, 478 U.S. 675 (1986), 54, 77, 80, 82

Board of Education, Island Trees Union Free School District No. 26 v. Pico by Pico, 457 U.S. 853 (1982), 80, 81

Brown v. Board of Education of Topeka (Brown I), 347 U.S. 483 (1954), 31

Brown v. Board of Education of Topeka (Brown II), 349 U.S. 294 (1955), 31

C

Connick v. Myers, 461 U.S. 138 (1983), 82

D

Dobbs v. Jackson Women's Health Organization, 597 U.S. 215 (2022), 171, 172

G

Garcetti v. Ceballos, 546 U.S. 410 (2006), 83

Gary B. v. Whitmer, No. 2: 16-cv-13292, (6th Cir. 2020), 32–34, 91, 104, 124, 134

Grimshaw v. Ford Motor Co., 119 Cal App 3d 757, 174 Cal Rptr 348 (1981), 13, 14

Grutter v. Bollinger, 539 U.S. 306 (2003), 90

© The Author(s), under exclusive license to Springer Nature Switzerland AG 2024
B. Godett, L. M. Nobile, *Exploring Administrative Decision-Making in Public Education*,
https://doi.org/10.1007/978-3-031-58782-5

H
Hazelwood School District v. Kuhlmeier, 484 U.S. 260 (1988), 81, 82

J
J.R. v. Hudson County Schools of Technology (HUD-L-3406-17), 14, 15

K
Kennedy v. Bremerton, 597 U.S. ___ (2022), 83, 84

L
Lander v. Seaver, 32 Vt. 114, 1859, 151
Leandro v. State, 488 S.E.2d 249 (1997), 92, 93, 96, 124, 127, 134
Liebeck v. McDonald's Restaurants, 1995 WL 360309, (D.C.N.M. 1994), 13, 14
Lujan v. Defenders of Wildlife (90-1424), 504 U.S. 555 (1992), 40

M
Mahanoy Area School District v. B.L., 594 U.S. ___ (2021), 78, 79, 151
McDougal v. Fox News Network, LLC, 489 F. Supp. 3d 174 (S.D.N.Y. 2020), 146
Meyer v. Nebraska, 262 U.S. 390 (1923), 29, 34, 69, 82
Minersville School District v. Gobitis, 310 U.S. 586 (1940), 29, 30, 32
Morse v. Frederick, 551 U.S. 393 (2007), 78, 79

P
Paradis v. Frost, 103 Mass. App. Ct. 410 (2023), 112, 113
Perez v. Sturgis Public Schools, 598 U.S. 142 (2023), 103
Peter W. v. San Francisco Unified School District, 60 Cal. App. 3d 815, 1976, 18, 49, 50, 53, 58, 64, 65, 102, 171
Pickering v. Board of Education, 391 U.S. 563 (1968), 82
Pierce v. Society of the Sisters, 268 U.S. 510 (1925), 28, 30, 34, 56, 69, 82
Pollack v. Regional School Unit 75, 886 F.3d 75 (1st Cir. 2018), 140, 141

R
Regents of the University of California v. Bakke, 438 U.S. 265 (1978), 88, 90
Roe v. Wade, 410 U.S. 113 (1973), 171

S
San Antonio v. Rodriguez, 411 U.S. 1 (1973), 134
Students for Fair Admissions v. President and Fellows of Harvard College, 600 U.S. 181 (2023), 90

T
Tinker v. Des Moines Independent Community School District, 393 U.S. 503 (1969), 20, 31, 54, 76–79
Troxel v. Granville, 530 U.S. 57 (2000), 56

CASE INDEX 175

W
West Virginia State Board of Education v. Barnette, 319 U.S. 624 (1943), 30
West Virginia v. Environmental Protection Agency, 597 U.S. ___ (2022), 132, 133
William Penn School District v. Pennsylvania Department of Education, No. 587 M.D. 2014 (2023), 28
Wisconsin v. Yoder, 406 U.S. 205 (1972), 31, 56, 69

Wyke v. Polk County School Board, 129 F.3d 560 (11th Cir. 1997), 110–113

Z
Z.Q. et al. v. New York City Department of Education et al, Z.Q. v. N.Y.C. Dep't of Educ., No. 1: 20-CV-9866-ALC, 2022 U.S. Dist. LEXIS 55956 (S.D.N.Y. Mar. 28, 2022), 124

Subject Index

A
Abortion, 43, 171
Academic freedom, 83
ACLU, 91, 92
Affirmative action, 88–90, 93
African American, 68, 93
Agencies, 18, 50, 55, 115, 132–133, 144, 161, 166
Aha!, 170, 172
Alaska, 78
Aldis, Judge Asa, 151
Amendment(s), 27, 28, 31, 69
American Council on the Teaching of Foreign Language (ACTFL), 128
American Federation of Teachers (AFT), 137
American Instructional Resources Survey, 161
Americans with Disabilities Act/ADA/ADA Amendments Act of 2008, 31, 104, 105, 141
Anti-bullying statutes, 114
Arizona, 64, 114

Artificial intelligence (AI), 58, 133, 158–161, 163–165
Assumptions, 19, 20, 51, 55, 76, 170, 172
Automation, 163, 167

B
Beliefs, 29, 30, 32, 41, 51, 55, 58, 66, 137, 164
Berger, Justice Warren E., 77
Biden, President Joseph Robinette, Jr., 3, 6, 89, 158
Bill of Rights, 28, 64
Biology, 57
Black, Derek, 83
Black, Justice Hugo, 20, 54
Blackstone, Judge Michael, 151
Blueprint for an AI Bill of Rights, 158
Bodily autonomy, 172
"Bong Hits 4 Jesus," 78
Book bans, 43, 75, 81, 82, 136, 149
Boston Latin School, 68
Brennan, Justice William J., 80

Breyer, Justice Stephen, 79
Brookings, 137
Bucks County, 135
Budget/budgetary, 50, 63, 64, 66, 163
Bullying, 15, 58, 95, 96, 113–115, 133
Burden of proof, 8, 9
Burger, Chief Justice Warren, 31

C
California, 13, 44, 102, 114, 170
Causal connection, 40
Cause of action, 8, 31, 102
Cell phones, 140, 142
Centers for Disease Control and Prevention (CDC), 44
Chaplains (unlicensed), 117
Charter schools, 18, 58, 117
ChatGPT, 158–160
Child Study Teams, 104
Chilling effect, 141
Choice, 42, 43, 58, 66, 69, 83, 88, 93–95, 116, 128, 135, 162, 171
Church and state, 83, 118
Civic(s), 32–34, 94, 95
Civil law, 7–9
Civil liberty, 30
Civil rights, 31, 91, 93, 95
Civil Rights Act of 1964, 88, 125
Coalition for Responsible Home Education (CRHE), 106
Committee on Oversight and Accountability (Oversight Committee), 144, 145
Common law negligence, 9, 10, 111
Community, 20, 21, 25, 31, 42, 50, 64, 66, 70, 76, 80, 93, 96, 116, 144, 145, 166
Computer, 114, 122, 123, 126, 160, 161

Confidentiality, 57
Conservative, 41–43, 69
Constitution, 27–29, 54, 66, 69, 77, 79–81, 83, 91, 101, 104, 127, 135–137, 163, 170
Court of public opinion, 9, 15, 43
COVID-19, 40, 41, 51–53, 97, 105, 106, 122–125, 127, 129, 133, 136, 140, 144, 145, 163, 165, 171
Criminal law, 7, 8
Critical race theory (CRT), 43, 94
Culture, 8, 51, 64
Curriculum/curricula, 34, 39, 41–44, 46, 51, 54, 56–58, 65, 69, 75, 80–83, 93, 94, 103, 105, 125, 127, 128, 132, 135, 136, 140, 142, 148, 149, 158–160, 162, 164, 165, 172

D
Damages, 10–13, 15, 22, 45, 104, 112, 123, 124
Darling-Hammond, Linda, 58, 166
Data, 53, 79, 106, 158–160, 164
Dear Colleague Letter, 125–127
Decision(s), 3, 9, 18, 19, 21, 22, 28–31, 33, 34, 40, 42, 51, 54, 56–58, 65, 70, 78, 80–84, 88, 90, 102–105, 115, 132–134, 136, 141, 170, 171
Deliberate indifference, 89, 162
Democracy, 19, 30, 32, 33, 54, 77, 79, 80, 94, 95, 134
Democrat(s)/democratic, 19, 33
Demographic(s), 88, 93, 94
Department of Education, 55, 89, 93, 94, 106, 107, 123, 124
Detroit, Michigan, 32, 91
Diaz, Manny, 134, 135
Digital resources, 125

Discrimination, 88, 90, 91, 96, 114, 126, 141
Dissent, 20, 30, 54, 83
District, 4, 15, 21–24, 31, 33, 34, 42, 49, 51, 64, 65, 84, 88, 89, 92–95, 97, 101, 103, 104, 106, 111–113, 115–118, 123–129, 134–136, 141, 145, 146, 160–163
District of Columbia, 43
Diverse/diversity, 66, 83, 90, 103, 128, 162, 165
"Don't Say Gay," 43, 70, 75
Due process, 28
Duties, 15

E

Education Freedom Center at the Independent Women's Forum, 145
Education Law Center, 66
Education reform, 52
EdWeek/Education Week, 53, 66, 69, 97, 163
Elementary and Secondary School Emergency Relief Fund (ESSER), 123
Elements of negligence
  breach, 4, 8–13, 15, 18, 19, 32, 43–45, 50, 76, 110, 122–124, 129, 147, 171
  causation, 4, 10–12, 45, 123, 124
  duty, 4, 6, 9–12, 15, 18–21, 32, 34, 35, 40, 43–45, 49, 50, 53, 55–58, 64, 65, 70, 76, 79–84, 95, 101, 104, 105, 109, 110, 113, 115, 117, 122, 123, 127–129, 136, 137, 146, 147, 151, 158, 161–167, 170–172
  injury, 4, 6, 8–13, 15, 19, 21, 22, 25, 29, 32, 34, 35, 40–42, 45, 50, 60, 80, 84, 96, 102, 104, 112, 115, 117, 122–125, 129, 158, 167, 171
"Emerging School Models," 106
English, 29, 68, 92, 151
English Language Learners, 103
Entertainment, 140, 146, 147
Entitlement, 4, 55, 101, 103, 105, 107, 171
Equal, 84, 87, 91–93, 125
Equality, 80, 87, 88
Equal protection, 66, 91, 158
Equity, 34, 80, 87–97, 166
Ethics, 55, 70
"Every Student Succeeds Act," 103
Expression, 30, 31, 34, 54, 75–84, 114

F

Fact Sheet, 158
Faculty speech, 82
Fair/fairly, 18, 81, 83, 87, 88, 122
Faith-based schools, 66, 69
Family law, 7, 8
First Amendment, 32, 58, 75, 76, 78, 79, 81, 83, 84, 118
First Circuit, 33, 95, 140
Flemington, New Jersey, 148
Florida, 44, 64, 70, 93, 94, 134–136, 170
Football, 83, 95, 111
Fortas, Justice Abraham, 76, 77
Fourteenth Amendment, 56, 91, 158
Frankfurter, Justice Felix, 30, 32, 34
Free appropriate public education (FAPE), 106, 107, 124
Freedom(s), 28, 30, 32, 70, 76, 77, 83, 170
Free exercise, 32, 34, 76, 84
Free expression, 30, 31, 34, 75–84
Free speech, 84, 133
Fundamental right(s), 28, 30–32, 56, 57, 76, 91, 92, 104, 170

Funding
  choice, 69
  declining population, 163
  homeschooling, 134, 163
  private schools, 64, 66, 69, 163
Future, 20, 28, 34, 50, 56, 96, 129, 134, 137, 157–167, 170, 171
FutureEd, 64
Futurists, 158, 163–166

G

Gender/gender identity/gender identities, 41, 44, 55, 57, 58, 65, 80, 114, 161, 162, 171
Georgetown University, 64
Georgia, 64
Gifted and talented (G&T), 91, 103
Gorsuch, Justice Neil, 83, 84
Governance, 51, 64, 66, 94, 131–137, 162, 163
Government, 8, 18, 19, 28, 65, 66, 76, 84, 103, 131–133, 146
Graham, Lindsey, 133
Guardians, 28, 44, 112, 170
Gun violence, 143

H

Harassment, 15, 88, 89, 111, 114
Harvard University, 90, 97, 106
Health, 29, 42, 43, 52, 57, 65, 105, 109–118, 136, 144, 145, 148, 149, 162, 171, 172
Higher order skills
  analysis, 79
  critical thinking, 79
Hillsdale College, 135
"Historical practices and understanding," 84
Homeschooling, 69, 106, 107, 134, 163
Horizon technologies, 161

I

I Am Jazz, 41, 42
Imaginative play, 140, 149
Individualized Education Plan (IEP), 103, 105
Individuals with Disabilities Education Act (IDEA), 31, 103–106, 124
Inflection point, 3, 4, 6, 160, 172
Influencer, 142
Infrastructure, 66, 125, 132
Injury in fact, 40–42, 45
In loco parentis, 20, 79, 150, 151
In-person instruction, 145, 146
Internet, 122, 123, 126, 127, 141, 142, 159, 160
Internet use, 160

J

Jackson, Justice Robert Houghwout, 30
Jennings, Jazz, 41
Jersey City, New Jersey, 93, 96
Judgment(s), 31, 55, 88, 151, 170
Jurisdiction, 170
Justice, 20, 29–34, 76–84, 97, 134

K

K-12, 12, 91, 94, 105, 110, 128, 161, 166, 171, 172
Kappan, 163, 166
Kennedy, Justice Anthony, 83

L

Legislation, 64–66, 70, 76, 82, 114, 117, 158, 161, 172
LGBTQ+, 42, 43, 116, 136
Liability, 4, 6, 8, 9, 17–19, 22, 24, 25, 33, 34, 50, 51, 58–60, 64, 75, 89, 102, 104–106, 118, 123,

SUBJECT INDEX 181

124, 126–128, 132, 133, 137, 143, 146, 147, 150, 158, 159, 167, 169, 172
Liberal, 43, 150
Liberty, 28–31, 151
Library, 41, 42, 64, 80, 81, 94
Literacy, 32, 33, 91, 102, 104, 124, 126, 160
Loudon County, 89
Louisiana, 64

M
Massachusetts, 113, 151
Massachusetts Teachers Association (MTA), 137
Materials, 41, 65, 80–82, 125, 143, 162, 165
McReynolds, Justice, 29
Media, 8, 43, 76, 78, 79, 92, 94, 109, 116, 139, 142, 144
Mental health, 52, 109–118
Michigan, 32, 91
Minority(ies), 82
Mississippi, 44
Model Policy(ies), 55–58
Moms for Liberty (M4L), 69, 136, 137
Montana, 113
Muñiz, Raquel, 171, 172

N
National Assessment of Educational Progress (NAEP), 52, 97, 145
National Association for Gifted Children (NAGC), 103
National Center for Education Statistics (NCES), 52, 110
National Education Association (NEA), 137
Negligence per se, 9, 10

Neighbor, 20, 21, 41, 42
New Jersey, 93, 115, 116, 142, 143, 148
News, 13, 146, 147
New York, 140, 147
New York City, 124
New York Times, 52, 133
Next-gen negligence, 6, 7, 15, 25, 34, 35, 39–46, 65, 75–84, 87–97, 101–107, 109–118, 121–129, 131–137, 139–152, 157–167, 169–171
North Carolina, 92, 148
Northwest Ordinance in 1787, 19

O
Obama, President Barack Hussein II, 103, 125
Office of Civil Rights (OCR), 125, 126, 132
Oklahoma, 69
Opinion, 9, 15, 29–31, 33, 34, 45, 49, 52, 77–80, 83, 84, 90, 95, 146, 147, 151, 159
Opt-in, 44, 65
Opt-out, 44, 149

P
Paradigms, 129
Parental rights/parents' rights, 29, 56, 57, 64–66, 69, 70, 136
Parental Rights in Education, 56, 70
Parents, 20, 22–25, 28, 29, 32, 34, 35, 39–41, 43–45, 51, 52, 54–58, 63–70, 76, 79–82, 84, 88, 96, 102, 104, 106, 107, 111–116, 124, 134, 135, 140–152, 159, 170, 171
Parochial school, 29, 134
Pedagogy, 79, 102, 103, 140, 144, 162, 165

PEN America, 70
Pennridge School District, 135
PEW Research, 146
Philadelphia, 135
Philadelphia Inquirer, 117
Physical conditions, 93
Pico, 80, 81
Policy, 33, 34, 44, 49–60, 78, 88, 95, 113–115, 126, 137, 159, 160, 162, 166, 172
Political speech, 77, 79
Powell, Justice Lewis F. Jr., 134
Precedent, 9, 10, 50, 51, 79, 80, 83, 105, 152
PreK-12, 89, 134
Preponderance of the evidence, 8, 10, 12
Press, 28, 52–54, 57, 76
Privacy, 55, 133, 158, 159
Private school, 64, 66, 69, 107, 116, 136, 163
Professional development, 60, 104, 167
PTA/PTO, 63
Public Interest Privacy Center, 159
Public opinion, 15, 43
Public policy, 17–21, 24, 25, 31–33, 49–60, 65, 102, 105, 171
Public school/public schooling/public education, 3, 4, 6, 9, 12, 14, 15, 18–21, 28–32, 39–45, 51–56, 58, 63–66, 68–70, 76, 78–80, 82–84, 88, 90–92, 94, 96, 97, 102, 103, 105–107, 110, 113, 116, 117, 123, 129, 131–137, 139, 140, 143–145, 147, 150, 157–167, 171

Q
Quality education, 58, 136
Quota, 88, 90

R
Race/racial, 30, 66, 68, 80, 88, 90, 91, 93, 114, 125, 126, 134, 161, 162
Race-based admissions, 90, 91
Rand Corporation, 161
Reasonably prudent, 12, 13
Relationships, 4, 19, 21, 24, 34, 42, 49, 50, 102, 113, 131, 140, 144, 148, 166, 167, 172
Religion, 19, 28, 32, 34, 76, 80, 83, 88, 92, 114
  holiday celebrations, 83
  pray, 83
  school prayer, 83
Religious organizations, 83
Republicans, 80
"Revolutionizers of Jersey City High Schools," 93
Rhode Island, 34, 94, 95
Roberts, Chief Justice John G., Jr., 30, 78, 90

S
Safe/safety, 11–13, 15, 19–21, 25, 32, 43, 45, 57, 58, 65, 75, 89, 91, 96, 110, 115, 117, 125, 137, 159
Safe Place to Learn Act, 114
Sanctions, 54, 77, 82
Scalia, Justice Antonin, 69
School board/school committee/board, 13, 15, 30, 31, 34, 42, 51, 52, 63, 64, 77, 80–82, 88, 93, 95, 111, 112, 116, 117, 135–137, 143, 146, 147, 162, 165
School district, 15, 34, 42, 92–95, 101, 106, 111–113, 116–118, 124, 126, 127, 136, 141, 145, 146, 160
Schoolhouse, 39, 76, 78, 79, 107, 122

School policy, 53, 55, 78
School programs, 64, 123
School shooting, 109, 116, 143
School-sponsored activities, 82
Scores, 53, 145
Secretary of Education, 133
Section 504 of the Rehabilitation Act of 1973, 31, 105
Select Subcommittee on the Coronavirus Pandemic, 144
Settlement, 33, 114
1776 Curriculum, 135
Sex education, 43, 44, 57
Sexuality Information and Education Council of the United States (SIECUS), 43, 44
Sexual orientation, 42, 44, 114
Shostak, Arthur, 165, 166
Sixth Circuit, 32, 33, 104
Slavery, 43
Smith, Judge William E., 33, 34
Snapchat, 79, 116
Social justice, 84
Social media, 76, 78, 79, 109, 116, 139, 142, 144
Social studies curriculum, 135
Society/societal, 6, 30, 32, 33, 55, 76, 77, 84, 90, 93, 117, 122, 127, 134, 161, 163, 166
Sotomayor, Justice Sonia, 83
Southern Poverty Law Center (SPLC), 136
Special education, 103, 105–107, 110, 117
Special needs, 103, 105–107, 124, 134
Special relationships, 19, 21, 113
Speech, 28, 54, 76–82, 84, 94, 133
Sports, 55, 63, 91, 93, 95, 106
Staffing, 91, 105
Stakeholder(s), 4, 21, 43, 45, 70, 137, 161, 165, 166, 170

Standing, 20, 34, 35, 40–43, 45, 79
Status quo, 25, 70
Stone, Justice Harlan, 30
"Stop W.O.K.E.," 94
Suicide, 110–113, 133, 145
Summary judgment, 170
Support, 33, 42, 52, 64, 79, 81, 91, 103–105, 115, 117, 125–128, 132–134, 141, 160–162, 165, 166, 172
Susskind, Daniel, 163–166

T
Take-aways, 76, 83, 170–172
Taxpayer, 35, 41, 43, 45, 54
Technology, 3, 6, 22, 39, 92, 114, 121–129, 139, 140, 158–161, 164, 165, 167
TED talks, 163
Teen Prevention Education Program (Teen PEP), 148, 149
Tenth Amendment, 27, 66
Texas, 117, 118, 142, 143
Texas Senate Bill 763, 117
TikTok, 142, 143
Tinker test, 77
Title IX of the Education Amendments of 1972, 88, 89, 93, 95, 96
Title VI of the Civil Rights Act of 1964, 125
Tort, 7–9, 40, 96, 102, 145
Tort Claims Act, 113
Tortfeasor, 9
Traditional negligence, 7, 40, 44, 45, 123
Transgender, 41, 42, 54, 55, 57, 58, 89, 96
Trauma, 105
Turning point, 3

U

U.S. Constitution, 27–29, 66, 83, 104, 170
U.S. Department of Education, 89, 93, 106, 107, 123, 124
U.S. Supreme Court, SCOTUS, 9, 15, 18, 28, 33, 40, 54, 78, 89, 104, 105, 133, 134, 151, 171
United States, 27–29, 33, 53, 54, 56, 64, 66, 76, 78, 83, 88, 89, 91, 93, 104–106, 110, 114, 124, 128, 132–134, 170, 171
University(ies), 83, 90, 91, 94, 110

V

Values, 31, 45, 51, 54, 77, 146, 147
Vermilion Education, 135
Vermont, 151, 170
Virginia, 55–57, 89, 145

Virtual learning/virtual schooling, 52, 122, 123, 144, 145, 165, 171
Voting Rights Act, 31

W

Warren, Elizabeth, 133
Washington, 20, 140
Washington Post, 106
Weishart, Joshua E., 170, 171
White, Justice Byron R., 81, 82
Whitmer, Governor Gretchen, 33, 104
Women's rights, 31, 171
Workforce, 149, 161–167
Workplace, 161–167

Z

Zoom, 40, 123

SPRINGER NATURE

GPSR Compliance

The European Union's (EU) General Product Safety Regulation (GPSR) is a set of rules that requires consumer products to be safe and our obligations to ensure this.

If you have any concerns about our products, you can contact us on ProductSafety@springernature.com

In case Publisher is established outside the EU, the EU authorized representative is:

Springer Nature Customer Service Center GmbH
Europaplatz 3
69115 Heidelberg, Germany

The manufacturer's authorised representative in the EU is Springer Nature Customer Service Centre GmbH, Europaplatz 3, 69115 Heidelberg, Germany. If you have any concerns regarding our products, please contact ProductSafety@springernature.com

Printed and bound by CPI Group (UK) Ltd, Croydon, CR0 4YY
23/03/2026
02076447-0001